A WORD A DAY

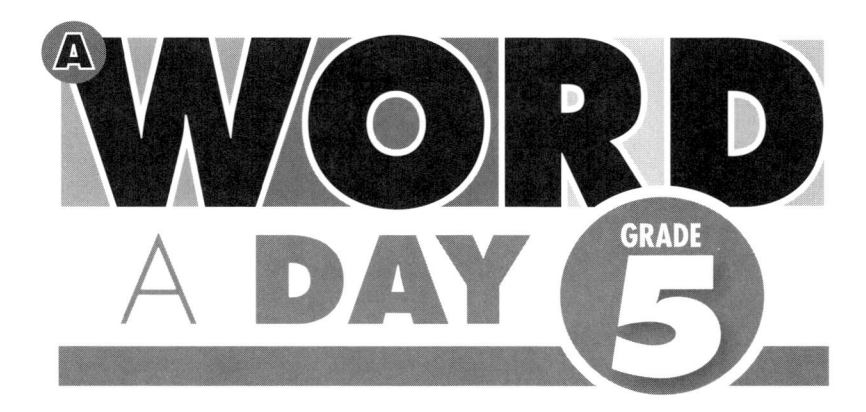

GRADE 5

Editorial Development: Marilyn Evans
Robyn Raymer
Sarita Chávez Silverman
Stephanie Wright
Copy Editing: Carrie Gwynne
Art Direction: Cheryl Puckett
Cover Design: David Price
Design/Production: Susan Bigger
John D. Williams

EMC 2795

Evan-Moor
EDUCATIONAL PUBLISHERS
Helping Children Learn since 1979

Congratulations on your purchase of some of the finest teaching materials in the world.

Photocopying the pages in this book is permitted for single-classroom use only. Making photocopies for additional classes or schools is prohibited.

For information about other Evan-Moor products, call 1-800-777-4362, fax 1-800-777-4332, or visit our Web site, www.evan-moor.com. Entire contents © 2009 EVAN-MOOR CORP. 18 Lower Ragsdale Drive, Monterey, CA 93940-5746. Printed in USA.

Correlated to State Standards
Visit *teaching-standards.com* to view a correlation of this book's activities to your state's standards. This is a free service.

Weekly Walk-Through

Each week of **A Word a Day** follows the same format, making it easy for both students and teacher to use.

Words of the Week

Four new words are presented each week. A definition, example sentence, and discussion prompts are provided for each word.

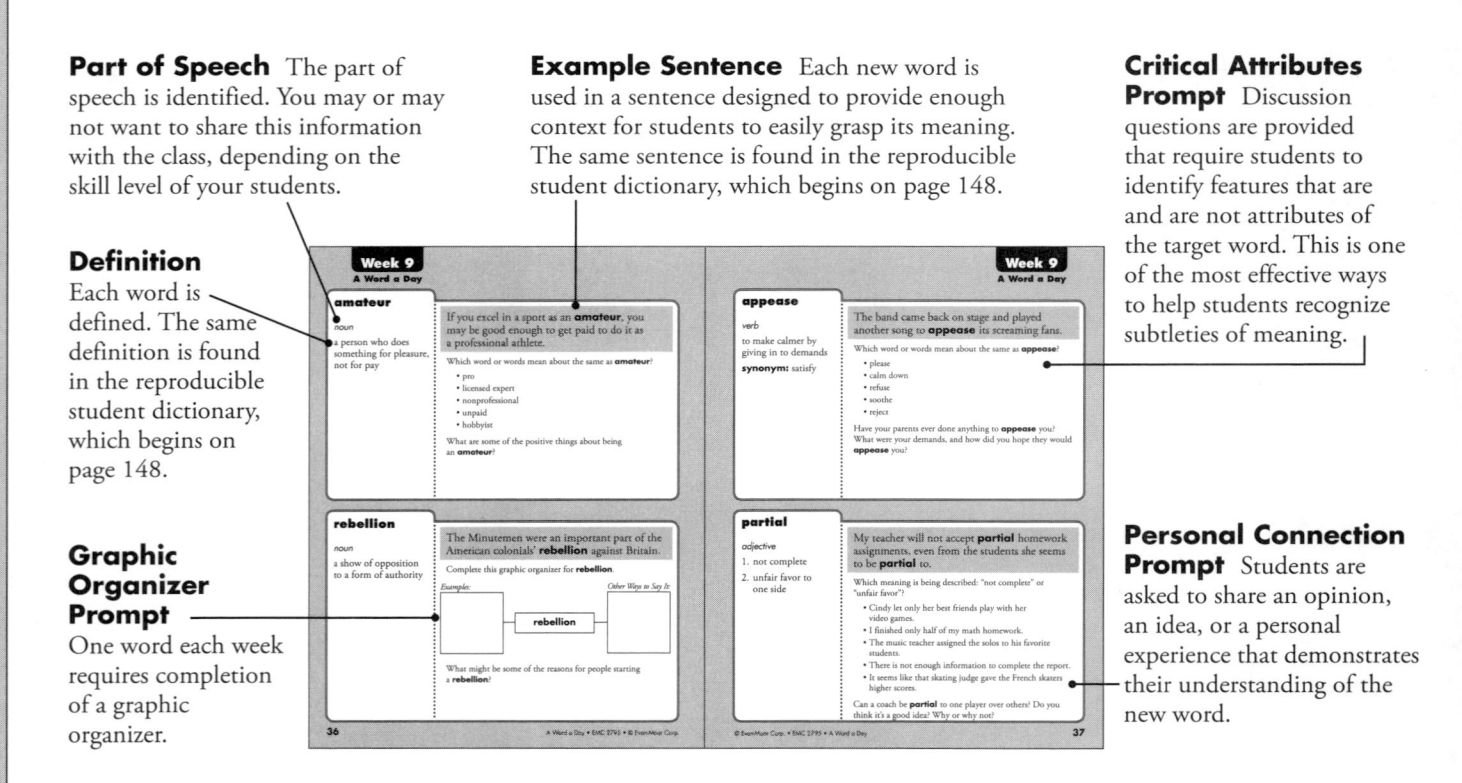

Part of Speech The part of speech is identified. You may or may not want to share this information with the class, depending on the skill level of your students.

Definition Each word is defined. The same definition is found in the reproducible student dictionary, which begins on page 148.

Graphic Organizer Prompt One word each week requires completion of a graphic organizer.

Example Sentence Each new word is used in a sentence designed to provide enough context for students to easily grasp its meaning. The same sentence is found in the reproducible student dictionary, which begins on page 148.

Critical Attributes Prompt Discussion questions are provided that require students to identify features that are and are not attributes of the target word. This is one of the most effective ways to help students recognize subtleties of meaning.

Personal Connection Prompt Students are asked to share an opinion, an idea, or a personal experience that demonstrates their understanding of the new word.

How to Present the Words

Use one of the following methods to present each word:

- Write the word on the board. Then read the definition and the example sentence, explaining as needed before conducting oral activities.

- Make an overhead transparency of the lesson page that shows the word. Then guide students through the definition, example sentence, and oral activities. Make a transparency of page 158 to use with lessons that feature a graphic organizer.

- Reproduce the dictionary on pages 148–157 for each student, or provide each student with a student practice book. (See inside front cover.) Have students find the word in their dictionary and then guide them through the definition, example sentence, and oral activities.

2 A Word a Day • EMC 2795 • © Evan-Moor Corp.

A WORD A DAY

End-of-Week Review

Review the four words of the week through oral and written activities designed to reinforce student understanding.

Oral Review
Four oral activities provide you with prompts to review the week's words.

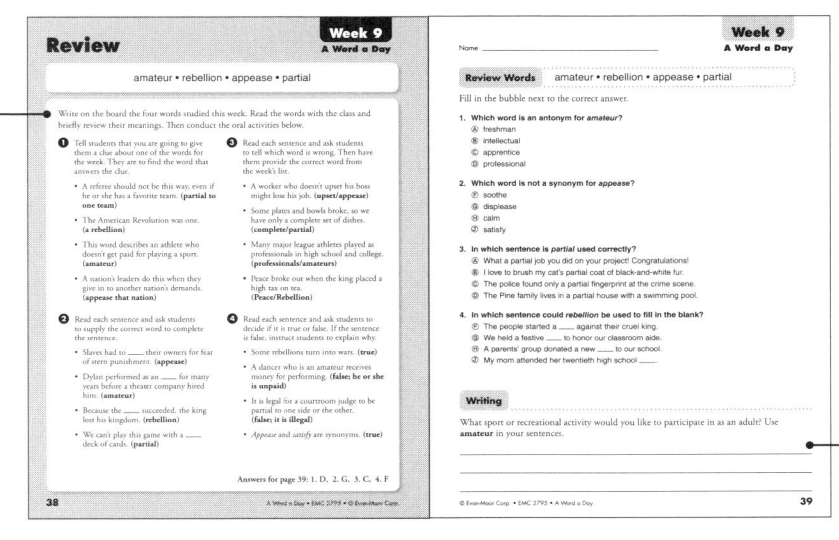

Written Assessment
A student reproducible containing four multiple-choice items and an open-ended writing activity can be used to assess students' mastery.

Additional Features

- Reproducible student dictionary
- Cumulative word index

Week 1
A Word a Day

elevate

verb

to raise or lift up

The mechanic had to **elevate** the car in order to have room to work underneath it.

Which of the following are examples of something being **elevated**?

- Place the flowerpot on top of bricks to get it up off the deck.
- Put the pot in the drawer under the stove.
- The riverside homes are built on high platforms.
- Hold little Annie on your shoulders so she can see the parade.
- The juggler performed amazing tricks while balancing on stilts.

If a friend is feeling blue, what might you do to **elevate** his or her spirits?

garland

noun

a ring of flowers or leaves; a wreath

A beautiful **garland** made of holly was used to decorate our front door.

Which of the following could describe a **garland**?

- fragrant
- leafy
- rocky
- floral
- colorful

What are some occasions when you might hang a **garland** in your home?

Week 1
A Word a Day

flammable

adjective

easily set on fire

The rags soaked in gasoline were extremely **flammable**.

Complete this graphic organizer for **flammable**.

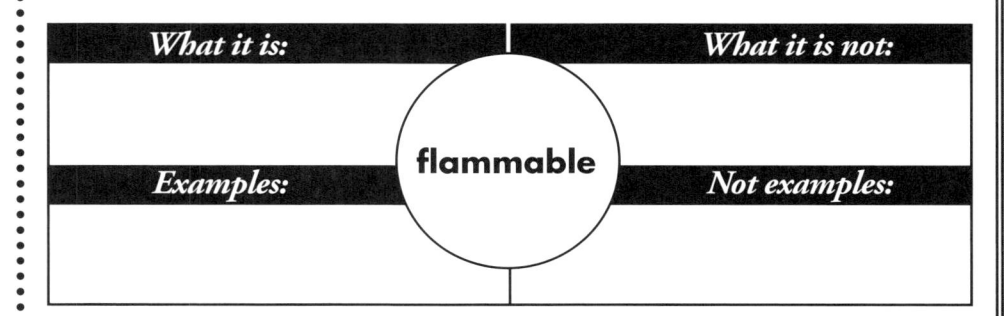

What it is:		What it is not:
Examples:	flammable	Not examples:

Where have you seen signs warning that something is **flammable**?

horde

noun

a large, moving crowd

synonym: swarm

A **horde** of spectators rushed from the stadium after the powerful earthquake.

Which words mean about the same as **horde**?

- big group
- couple
- multitude
- trio
- mob

In what type of situations might you see a **horde**?

Review

Week 1
A Word a Day

elevate • garland • flammable • horde

Write on the board the four words studied this week. Read the words with the class and briefly review their meanings. Then conduct the oral activities below.

❶ Tell students that you are going to give them a clue about one of the words for the week. They are to find the word that answers the clue.

- You could use this word to describe gasoline. **(flammable)**
- On a holiday, people often hang one of these on their front door. **(a garland)**
- When you lift something, you do this to it. **(elevate it)**
- You could use this word to name a crowd of people who are all waiting to get into a sports stadium. **(horde)**

❷ Read each sentence and ask students to supply the correct word to complete the sentence.

- Dry grass is extremely ____. **(flammable)**
- Outside the water park, a ____ of visitors waited to get in. **(horde)**
- Please ____ the couch so I can move the rug. **(elevate)**
- As a bridesmaid at her cousin's wedding, Emma wore a ____ of flowers on her head. **(garland)**

❸ Read each sentence and ask students to tell which word is wrong. Then have them provide the correct word from the week's list.

- A crane will lower this steel bar to the top of the skyscraper. **(lower/elevate)**
- Cheering as they ran, a pair of fans swarmed onto the football field. **(pair/horde)**
- Move those fireproof materials away from the campfire. **(fireproof/flammable)**

❹ Read each sentence and ask students to decide if it is true or false. If the sentence is false, instruct students to explain why.

- When you elevate your foot, you lower it. **(false; when you elevate something, you raise it)**
- "A few people" is the same as a horde. **(false; a horde is a crowd)**
- Flammable materials can be very dangerous. **(true)**
- A girl may wear a garland on a special occasion. **(true)**

Answers for page 7: 1. B, 2. G, 3. B, 4. H

Name _____

Week 1
A Word a Day

Review Words   elevate • garland • flammable • horde

Fill in the bubble next to the correct answer.

1. Which word is an antonym for *elevate*?
   Ⓐ excuse
   Ⓑ lower
   Ⓒ dislike
   Ⓓ revise

2. In which sentence is *horde* used correctly?
   Ⓕ I have such a horde of homework to do this weekend.
   Ⓖ A horde of hungry ants swarmed into the picnic basket.
   Ⓗ I met a friend, and then the horde of us went to a movie.
   Ⓙ There's a horde of dirty socks under your bed—pick them up!

3. In which sentence could *flammable* be used to fill in the blank?
   Ⓐ Bo has a ____ personality, so most people like him.
   Ⓑ As grass and leaves dry, they become more ____.
   Ⓒ Eva and Ana had a ____ argument today at school.
   Ⓓ Using ____ ink, I wrote my name on my soccer ball.

4. Which phrase describes a *garland*?
   Ⓕ a ring of people holding hands
   Ⓖ a wedding or an engagement ring
   Ⓗ a decorative ring of flowers
   Ⓙ a loud doorbell

Writing

Write about a time when you were part of a horde. Use **horde** in your sentences.

_____

_____

_____

Week 2
A Word a Day

immaculate

adjective

extremely clean and neat

I've spent all morning cleaning my bedroom, and now it is **immaculate**.

Complete this graphic organizer for **immaculate**.

Examples: — **immaculate** — *Other Ways to Say It:*

Why is it important for a restaurant kitchen to be **immaculate**?

junction

noun

a place where things meet or cross

We live at the **junction** of Main Street and Maple Avenue.

Where can you find a **junction**?

- on major roadways
- in the ocean
- on railroad tracks
- on a beach
- in the sky

What is a **junction** near your home?

Week 2
A Word a Day

yearn
verb

to have a strong wish or longing for something

After she moved to a new school, Margo missed her old friends and **yearned** to see them again.

Which words mean about the same as **yearn**?

- want
- detest
- desire
- dislike
- long for

What would you **yearn** for if you didn't have it anymore?

collate
verb

to put pages together in the correct order

When the pages of my report got mixed up, I had to **collate** them.

Which of the following would you need to **collate**?

- pages of a picture dictionary that you made
- a stack of flyers
- pages to make a calendar
- pages in a paperback book
- articles written by different people for a school magazine

How would you figure out how to **collate** the pages in a class dictionary?

Review

Week 2
A Word a Day

immaculate • junction • yearn • collate

Write on the board the four words studied this week. Read the words with the class and briefly review their meanings. Then conduct the oral activities below.

❶ Tell students that you are going to give them a clue about one of the words for the week. They are to find the word that answers the clue.

- This is a place where two roads intersect. **(a junction)**

- You'd probably do this if your best friend moved away. **(yearn for that person)**

- If you dropped a loose-leaf notebook and all of the numbered pages spilled out, you'd have to do this. **(collate them)**

- This word describes a spotless, snow-white sheet. **(immaculate)**

❷ Read each sentence and ask students to supply the correct word to complete the sentence.

- Our Uncle Joe is so much fun, we ___ for his next visit. **(yearn)**

- Three-year-old Ana's party dress was ___ at first, but she soon got it dirty. **(immaculate)**

- Turn right at the ___ of Sage and Basil Lanes. **(junction)**

- These pages are out of order; please ___ them. **(collate)**

❸ Read each sentence and ask students to tell which word or words are wrong. Then have them provide the correct word from the week's list.

- Here, let me mix up those pages before you read them. **(mix up/collate)**

- I hate to see my grandparents again. **(hate/yearn)**

- The bride looked lovely in her grubby white dress. **(grubby/immaculate)**

❹ Read each sentence and ask students to decide if it is true or false. If the sentence is false, instruct students to explain why.

- *Junction* and *intersection* are synonyms. **(true)**

- An immaculate sweater needs cleaning. **(false; it is already perfectly clean)**

- Shuffling cards is the same as collating them. **(false; shuffling is the opposite of collating)**

- When their owners go on vacation, many dogs yearn for them. **(true)**

Answers for page 11: 1. D, 2. F, 3. C, 4. G

Name _____

Week 2
A Word a Day

Review Words immaculate • junction • yearn • collate

Fill in the bubble next to the correct answer.

1. Which word is a synonym for *junction*?
   Ⓐ sidewalk
   Ⓑ railroad
   Ⓒ highway
   Ⓓ crossroads

2. Which word is an antonym for *immaculate*?
   Ⓕ filthy
   Ⓖ crowded
   Ⓗ colorful
   Ⓙ empty

3. In which sentence could *collate* be used to fill in the blank?
   Ⓐ After I ____ the trash, I can watch a movie with you.
   Ⓑ If you ____ your hair every day, it will be clean and shiny.
   Ⓒ After I dropped my report, I had to ____ the pages.
   Ⓓ Please come and ____ your dinner before it gets cold.

4. Which sentence describes people who *yearn* for a vacation?
   Ⓕ We're having a fabulous time! We wish you were here!
   Ⓖ All year, we've been longing to get away on vacation.
   Ⓗ Last summer, we had a wonderful time at the beach.
   Ⓙ We just returned from our trip. It's great to be back home.

Writing

Write about something that always looks clean. Use **immaculate** in your sentences.

_____
_____
_____

© Evan-Moor Corp. • EMC 2795 • A Word a Day

Week 3
A Word a Day

tuition

noun

money paid to attend a school or college

My sister is saving all the money from her summer job for college **tuition**.

For which of the following might you pay **tuition**?
- a private school
- entrance to Disney World
- a weekend computer class
- classes at your local community college
- an airplane ticket

What options do students have if their parents can't afford **tuition** for college?

tamper

verb

to interfere with something so as to damage or change it

In some countries, it is common for candidates to **tamper** with the voting ballots in order to win an election.

Which word or words mean about the same as **tamper**?
- mess with
- leave alone
- change
- meddle
- respect

How are medicines and some other products packaged to prevent people from **tampering** with them?

Week 3
A Word a Day

vigorous

adjective

energetic, lively, and full of strength

We played a **vigorous** game of kickball at recess.

Which of the following activities are **vigorous**?

- running
- fishing
- writing
- bicycling
- dancing

Name some **vigorous** activities that you enjoy.

flourish

verb

to grow or develop in a strong and healthy way

We hope our tomato plants will **flourish** in the rich soil.

Complete this graphic organizer for **flourish**.

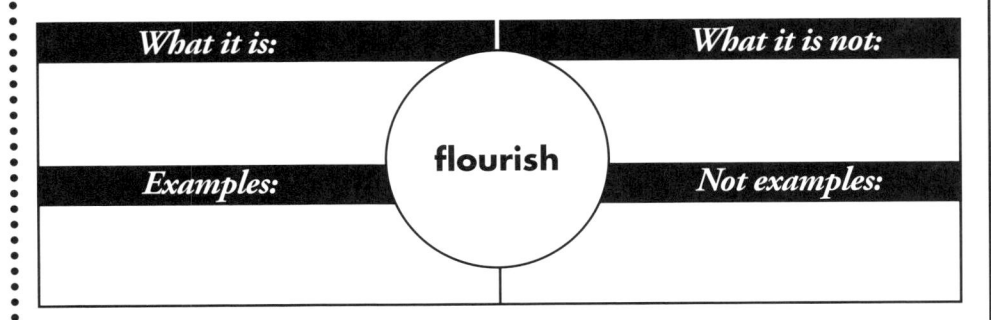

What it is:	What it is not:
	flourish	
Examples:	Not examples:

What are some things you can do to help plants **flourish**?

Review

Week 3
A Word a Day

tuition • tamper • vigorous • flourish

Write on the board the four words studied this week. Read the words with the class and briefly review their meanings. Then conduct the oral activities below.

1 Tell students that you are going to give them a clue about one of the words for the week. They are to find the word that answers the clue.

- This word describes what strong, healthy babies do as they grow. **(flourish)**
- Criminals who create computer viruses do this to other people's computers. **(tamper with them)**
- This is what students pay to attend college. **(tuition)**
- You might use this word to describe a soccer game. **(vigorous)**

2 Read each sentence and ask students to supply the correct word to complete the sentence.

- Holly's thick, curly hair requires ____ brushing. **(vigorous)**
- It is illegal to ____ with parking meters. **(tamper)**
- Steve's parents pay his school ____ at the beginning of each semester. **(tuition)**
- With a good diet and exercise, your puppy will ____. **(flourish)**

3 Read each sentence and ask students to tell which word is wrong. Then have them provide the correct word from the week's list.

- When you take good care of them, plants die. **(die/flourish)**
- In order to steal information, a hacker played with the company computer. **(played/tampered)**
- To get all the dust out of it, I gave the rug a weak shake. **(weak/vigorous)**

4 Read each sentence and ask students to decide if it is true or false. If the sentence is false, instruct students to explain why.

- Most public schools charge tuition. **(false; public schools are free)**
- Most plants flourish without water. **(false; most will die without water)**
- Strong, healthy people can handle vigorous exercise. **(true)**
- It is illegal to tamper with other people's property. **(true)**

Answers for page 15: 1. C, 2. J, 3. B, 4. H

Week 3
A Word a Day

Name _____

Review Words tuition • tamper • vigorous • flourish

Fill in the bubble next to the correct answer.

1. **Which word is a synonym for *vigorous*?**
   - Ⓐ fascinating
   - Ⓑ humorous
   - Ⓒ energetic
   - Ⓓ puzzling

2. **Which word is an antonym for *flourish*?**
   - Ⓕ relax
   - Ⓖ inflate
   - Ⓗ twist
   - Ⓙ weaken

3. **In which sentence could *tamper* be used to fill in the blank?**
   - Ⓐ Mom and Dad usually ____ with nonstick pans.
   - Ⓑ It is illegal to ____ with other people's mailboxes.
   - Ⓒ In Asian restaurants, I try to ____ with chopsticks.
   - Ⓓ Please don't ____ with the dog until after dinner.

4. **Which sentence describes college *tuition*?**
   - Ⓕ My cousin lives in a college dormitory that has 15 floors.
   - Ⓖ Shelby takes college courses in electrical engineering.
   - Ⓗ Some universities charge thousands of dollars a year.
   - Ⓙ In four years, Shelby will graduate and get a good job.

Writing

Write about a college that you have heard of. Guess how much it costs to attend that college. Use **tuition** in your sentences.

_____

_____

_____

Week 4
A Word a Day

snob

noun

a person who feels he or she is better than others

Michael is such a **snob**. He's always bragging about his expensive clothes and toys.

Which of these describe a **snob**?

- expects to be waited on by others
- treats everyone with kindness
- brags about possessions and accomplishments
- is eager to do extra work in a group project
- only wants to wear clothes with designer labels

How would you explain to a **snob** that people are all equal?

congested

adjective

1. to be overcrowded or filled to overflowing
2. having too much mucus in a body part

We drove to the pharmacy to get medicine for my **congested** sinuses. It took a long time because it was rush hour and the streets were **congested** with traffic.

Which meaning is being described: "overcrowded" or "filled with mucus"?

- I had such a bad cold that I used an entire box of tissues!
- At 5:30 p.m., the check-out area at the market is wall-to-wall shopping carts.
- We got stuck in bumper-to-bumper traffic this morning.
- I had a hard time sleeping because I couldn't breathe through my nose.
- It seemed like every kid in school was in the hallway.

Which places in our town get **congested**?

Week 4
A Word a Day

blotch

noun

a large spot or stain

The grape juice left a dark **blotch** on the white carpet.

Complete this graphic organizer for **blotch**.

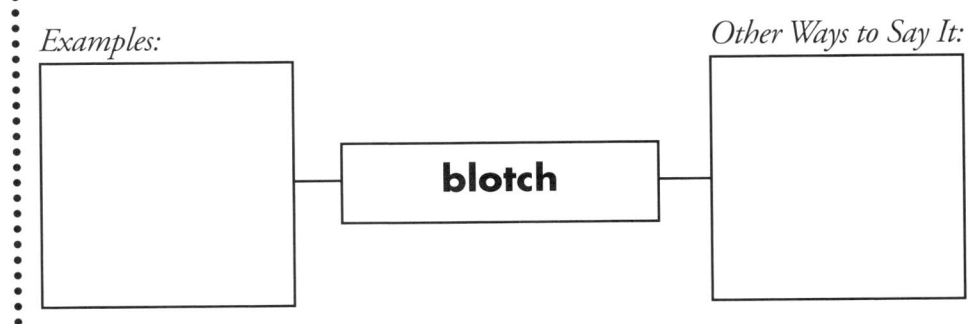

Examples: *Other Ways to Say It:*

blotch

What might you do to hide a **blotch** on a carpet?

automatic

adjective

operating without a person's control

In the past, we had to pour water in trays and freeze it to make ice, but now we have a new refrigerator with an **automatic** ice maker.

Which of the following items are **automatic**?

- an electric dishwasher
- a broom
- scissors
- an electric can opener
- motion-sensitive lights

What is something **automatic** that helps you do chores or work?

Review

Week 4
A Word a Day

snob • congested • blotch • automatic

Write on the board the four words studied this week. Read the words with the class and briefly review their meanings. Then conduct the oral activities below.

1 Tell students that you are going to give them a clue about one of the words for the week. They are to find the word that answers the clue.

- This word describes your nose when you have a bad cold. **(congested)**
- This word describes most kitchen appliances. **(automatic)**
- You wouldn't want one on your brand-new pants. **(a blotch)**
- This kind of person looks down on other people. **(a snob)**

2 Read each sentence and ask students to supply the correct word to complete the sentence.

- Three-year-old Rafael has a ____ of grape juice on his shirt. **(blotch)**
- The bridge was so ____ with traffic that it took an hour to cross it. **(congested)**
- Don't be such a ____! You're no better than the rest of us. **(snob)**
- In the early 1900s, kitchens did not have ____ dishwashers or microwaves. **(automatic)**

3 Read each sentence and ask students to tell which word or words are wrong. Then have them provide the correct word from the week's list.

- It takes longer to drive home when the streets are deserted. **(deserted/congested)**
- Our electric can opener is completely hand operated. **(hand operated/automatic)**
- That friendly person makes fun of me for wearing cheap shoes. **(friendly person/snob)**

4 Read each sentence and ask students to decide if it is true or false. If the sentence is false, instruct students to explain why.

- Most banks have automatic teller machines, or ATMs. **(true)**
- When your nose is congested, you have to breathe through your mouth. **(true)**
- A snob thinks everyone else is better than him or her. **(false; the opposite is true)**
- A blotch is hard to see. **(false; a blotch is quite visible)**

Answers for page 19: 1. D, 2. F, 3. B, 4. H

Week 4
A Word a Day

Name _____

Review Words   snob • congested • blotch • automatic

Fill in the bubble next to the correct answer.

1. Which word is a synonym for *congested*?
   - Ⓐ overjoyed
   - Ⓑ overanxious
   - Ⓒ overcritical
   - Ⓓ overcrowded

2. Which word or phrase means the opposite of *automatic*?
   - Ⓕ hand operated
   - Ⓖ homemade
   - Ⓗ complicated
   - Ⓙ computer generated

3. In which sentence could *blotch* be used to fill in the blank?
   - Ⓐ Please set this ____ on the dining room table.
   - Ⓑ There's a ____ of spaghetti sauce on my T-shirt.
   - Ⓒ This ____ will look great with your new jeans.
   - Ⓓ Mom bought a sofa and ____ for our living room.

4. Which sentence describes a *snob*?
   - Ⓕ Emily gave me part of her lunch because I'd left mine on the bus.
   - Ⓖ Pablo has two or three friends with whom he eats lunch at school.
   - Ⓗ Brandy looks down on people from neighborhoods other than hers.
   - Ⓙ Max enjoys being alone. He likes to work on his computer and read.

Writing

Write about a task you'd like to have a machine do for you. Use **automatic** in your sentences.

_____

_____

_____

Week 5
A Word a Day

glutton

noun

someone who eats and drinks greedily

An all-you-can-eat restaurant is the perfect place for a **glutton**.

Complete this graphic organizer for **glutton**.

Examples: → **glutton** ← *Other Ways to Say It:*

Have you ever eaten like a **glutton**? What made you eat that way? How did you feel afterward?

implore

verb

to beg urgently

synonym: plead

It doesn't matter how much we **implore**—our mother never lets us rent PG-13 movies.

Which of the following words mean about the same as **implore**?

- command
- plead
- pray
- demand
- request

What would you say to **implore** a parent to allow you to stay up late?

Week 5
A Word a Day

harmonious

adjective

being in agreement; peaceful

After the argument was settled, a **harmonious** feeling returned to the class.

Which of the following describe something **harmonious**?

- an orchestra playing together
- a heated debate in the halls of Congress
- a lakeshore at sunset, with insects buzzing and birds chirping
- preschool children arguing over toys in a sandbox
- a team of Alaskan huskies pulling a sled over the snow

What can you do to help make your classroom a **harmonious** place?

deplete

verb

to use up

Buying those expensive basketball shoes will **deplete** my savings.

Which of the following is it possible to **deplete**?

- underground deposits of oil
- money in a bank account
- water from the ocean
- grain stored in a silo
- tears from your eyes

Name some things at home or school that can be **depleted**.

Review

Week 5
A Word a Day

glutton • implore • harmonious • deplete

Write on the board the four words studied this week. Read the words with the class and briefly review their meanings. Then conduct the oral activities below.

❶ Tell students that you are going to give them a clue about one of the words for the week. They are to find the word that answers the clue.

- You might do this when you need help very badly. **(implore someone to help you)**
- This kind of person eats way too much. **(a glutton)**
- We shouldn't do this to Earth's natural resources. **(deplete them)**
- This word describes a family that enjoys playing games together. **(harmonious)**

❷ Read each sentence and ask students to supply the correct word to complete the sentence.

- What a ____ scene: all three of my cats are sleeping beside my dog. **(harmonious)**
- "Count Carl, I ____ you to release my father," the princess begged. **(implore)**
- Don't be such a ____! Save some food for others. **(glutton)**
- There hasn't been much rain, so we must take care not to ____ our water supply. **(deplete)**

❸ Read each sentence and ask students to tell which word or words are wrong. Then have them provide the correct word from the week's list.

- If you add to your savings, you'll have nothing left. **(add to/deplete)**
- I love parties that include lots of arguing people. **(arguing/harmonious)**
- Sam is a light eater who can wolf down a whole pie in one sitting. **(light eater/glutton)**
- "I command you to give me some food," begged the starving man. **(command/implore)**

❹ Read each sentence and ask students to decide if it is true or false. If the sentence is false, instruct students to explain why.

- *Implore* and *plead* are synonyms. **(true)**
- It is very unhealthy to eat like a glutton every day. **(true)**
- Lack of sleep can deplete a person's energy. **(true)**
- If a situation is harmonious, there is fighting and arguing. **(false; a harmonious situation is peaceful)**

Answers for page 23: 1. C, 2. F, 3. C, 4. F

Name _____

Week 5
A Word a Day

Review Words   glutton • implore • harmonious • deplete

Fill in the bubble next to the correct answer.

1. **Which word is a synonym for *deplete*?**
   - Ⓐ stretch
   - Ⓑ gather
   - Ⓒ empty
   - Ⓓ inflate

2. **Which phrase means the opposite of being a *glutton*?**
   - Ⓕ eats like a bird
   - Ⓖ eats like a horse
   - Ⓗ eats like a pig
   - Ⓙ eats like there's no tomorrow

3. **Which word is a synonym for *implore*?**
   - Ⓐ query
   - Ⓑ inform
   - Ⓒ beg
   - Ⓓ discourage

4. **What happens at a *harmonious* gathering?**
   - Ⓕ Everyone gets along well.
   - Ⓖ Everyone argues.
   - Ⓗ Everyone has a different idea.
   - Ⓙ Everyone wants to leave.

Writing

Write about a place where you feel peaceful. Use **harmonious** in your sentences.

_____

_____

_____

Week 6
A Word a Day

rendezvous

noun

a place for meeting

verb

to meet at a previously arranged time and place

> The playground was a popular **rendezvous** for the girls on the basketball team. They planned to **rendezvous** there right after school.

Which places might be a **rendezvous** for a sports team?

- a dark alley
- a pizza parlor
- the school gymnasium
- the museum of natural history
- a stadium

Name a place in our town that is a good **rendezvous** for people your age.

ponder

verb

to think about something very carefully

> You should take some time to **ponder** the question before writing your response.

Which of these mean about the same as **ponder**?

- ignore
- consider
- give it some thought
- brush off
- think over
- contemplate

What is something you have had to **ponder**?

Week 6
A Word a Day

noxious

adjective

harmful to the health of living beings

They evacuated the workers from the factory after a **noxious** chemical spilled.

Complete this graphic organizer for **noxious**.

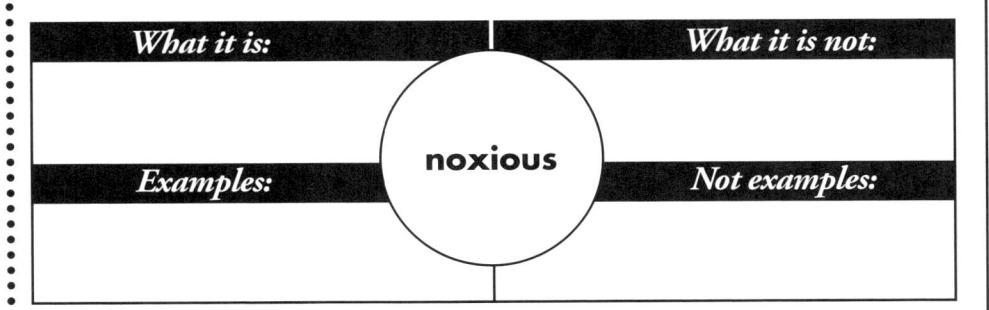

What it is:	What it is not:
Examples:	Not examples:

(noxious)

Name some products in your home that could be **noxious**.

quagmire

noun

1. soft, wet, soggy ground
2. a difficult situation; a predicament

When the trail led us to the edge of a **quagmire**, we were in a **quagmire** about how to get around the large, muddy area.

Which meaning is being described: "soggy ground" or "a difficult situation"?

- Your shoe was sucked off by the mud.
- The car was stuck up to its bumpers.
- Our neighbor's dog keeps digging up our flowers and we don't know how to tell them.
- Put on your boots to walk in the pasture.
- I told one friend that I'd go to the movies on Saturday, and I told another friend I'd go on a bike ride.

Tell about a time when you were in a **quagmire**. How did you resolve the predicament?

© Evan-Moor Corp. • EMC 2795 • A Word a Day

Review

Week 6
A Word a Day

rendezvous • ponder • noxious • quagmire

Write on the board the four words studied this week. Read the words with the class and briefly review their meanings. Then conduct the oral activities below.

1 Tell students that you are going to give them a clue about one of the words for the week. They are to find the word that answers the clue.

- You might do this when you have an important choice to make. **(ponder your choices)**
- People do this when they arrange to meet at a certain time and place. **(rendezvous)**
- This is a situation that is hard to get out of. **(a quagmire)**
- This word describes a poisonous snake's venom. **(noxious)**

2 Read each sentence and ask students to supply the correct word to complete the sentence.

- A black widow's bite is quite ___. **(noxious)**
- In the winter, the low places in our yard turn into a ___. **(quagmire)**
- Let me ___ for a few days before I make a decision. **(ponder)**
- Marley's Cafe is a popular ___ for college students because it's near the school. **(rendezvous)**

3 Read each sentence and ask students to tell which word is wrong. Then have them provide the correct word from the week's list.

- Since this is an important issue, I will ignore it. **(ignore/ponder)**
- It's hard to keep your feet dry when you're walking through a desert. **(desert/quagmire)**
- A healthy chemical in the water supply made many people sick. **(healthy/noxious)**

4 Read each sentence and ask students to decide if it is true or false. If the sentence is false, instruct students to explain why.

- *Meet* and *rendezvous* are synonyms. **(true)**
- Rattlesnakes have noxious venom. **(true)**
- People usually want to avoid a situation that is a quagmire. **(true)**
- Pondering takes less time than making a snap decision. **(false; when you ponder, you take time to think carefully)**

Answers for page 27: 1. D, 2. J, 3. A, 4. G

Name _____

Week 6
A Word a Day

Review Words rendezvous • ponder • noxious • quagmire

Fill in the bubble next to the correct answer.

1. **Which word is a synonym for *ponder*?**
   - Ⓐ explain
   - Ⓑ reject
   - Ⓒ forget
   - Ⓓ consider

2. **Which of these is a *quagmire*?**
   - Ⓕ Your friends all want to go out for pizza.
   - Ⓖ Your friends like to see the same movies.
   - Ⓗ Your friends pooled their money and bought you a birthday present.
   - Ⓙ Your friends want you to take sides in an argument.

3. **Which word is an antonym for *noxious*?**
   - Ⓐ harmless
   - Ⓑ flammable
   - Ⓒ frozen
   - Ⓓ liquid

4. **What happens at a *rendezvous*?**
   - Ⓕ People shop for food.
   - Ⓖ Two or more people meet.
   - Ⓗ People pass by on their way to other places.
   - Ⓙ People get on and off trains or buses.

Writing

Write about a decision that you had to consider very carefully. Use **ponder** in your sentences.

_____

_____

© Evan-Moor Corp. • EMC 2795 • A Word a Day   **27**

Week 7
A Word a Day

whimsical

adjective

odd or playful

synonym: fanciful

> We had to smile at the **whimsical** calendar photographs of dogs wearing clothing.

Which words mean about the same as **whimsical**?

- lighthearted
- serious
- imaginative
- amusing
- common

Describe a **whimsical** sight you have seen or a story you have read that had **whimsical** happenings.

killjoy

noun

a person who spoils the fun of others

> Marcy was a **killjoy** when she insisted on telling us how fattening and unhealthful the chocolate dessert was.

Which of these describe a **killjoy**? Someone who:

- says you won't enjoy the movie you're about to see
- works with you to plan a surprise party for a friend
- raves about the paintings you'll see at an exhibit
- lists all the diseases you might catch on your foreign vacation
- tells you who did it before you finish reading a mystery novel

How can you help a **killjoy** to act more positively?

Week 7
A Word a Day

versatile

adjective

able to do many different things well

Raul is a **versatile** athlete who can run, throw, and kick very well.

Which words mean about the same as **versatile**?

- rigid
- flexible
- adaptable
- unchanging
- multitalented

An object is **versatile** if it has a number of uses. What are some **versatile** objects you use?

convertible

noun

an automobile with a top that can be folded back or removed

adjective

able to be changed

Even with the top down on the **convertible**, we couldn't fit the **convertible** sofa bed in the car.

Which meaning is being described: "an automobile" or "able to be changed"?

- Mark's new car is perfect for driving on hot, sunny days.
- This jacket can be worn with either the red side or the blue side out.
- That sofa can be turned into a double bed.
- Sheila's scarf blew off her head while she was driving with the top down.
- It's starting to rain. Let's stop and put the top up.

What is something you own, or would like to own, that is **convertible**?

Review

Week 7
A Word a Day

whimsical • killjoy • versatile • convertible

Write on the board the four words studied this week. Read the words with the class and briefly review their meanings. Then conduct the oral activities below.

1 Tell students that you are going to give them a clue about one of the words for the week. They are to find the word that answers the clue.

- This word describes someone with many different skills and talents. **(versatile)**
- This is someone who's likely to spoil your fun. **(a killjoy)**
- This word describes a thing that is unusual and very imaginative. **(whimsical)**
- This word describes a couch that can be made into a bed. **(convertible)**

2 Read each sentence and ask students to supply the correct word to complete the sentence.

- I love to ride with the top down in my uncle's ___. **(convertible)**
- Jill is so ___ that I wonder if there's anything she can't do. **(versatile)**
- Only a ___ would spoil the party for the rest of us. **(killjoy)**
- One of the characters in this fantasy is a ___ talking teapot. **(whimsical)**

3 Read each sentence and ask students to tell which word or words are wrong. Then have them provide the correct word from the week's list.

- We laughed and laughed at the serious animated film. **(serious/whimsical)**
- Mandy is such a joyful person that she ruins every party she attends. **(joyful person/killjoy)**
- When you ride in a hardtop, you can feel the breeze blowing through your hair. **(hardtop/convertible)**

4 Read each sentence and ask students to decide if it is true or false. If the sentence is false, instruct students to explain why.

- *Whimsical* and *fanciful* are antonyms. **(false; they are synonyms)**
- A killjoy is a very desirable party guest. **(false; a killjoy spoils everyone's fun)**
- A versatile athlete is good at many sports. **(true)**
- A convertible jacket is handy for travel. **(true)**

Answers for page 31: 1. C, 2. H, 3. D, 4. H

Name _____

Week 7
A Word a Day

Review Words whimsical • killjoy • versatile • convertible

Fill in the bubble next to the correct answer.

1. **Which word is a synonym for *versatile*?**
   - Ⓐ carpeted
   - Ⓑ choral
   - Ⓒ multitalented
   - Ⓓ multicolored

2. **What can you do in a *convertible* that you can't do in other cars?**
   - Ⓕ drive on unpaved roads
   - Ⓖ drive over 65 miles per hour
   - Ⓗ drive with the top down
   - Ⓙ drive on winding roads

3. **Which phrase means the opposite of *killjoy*?**
   - Ⓐ bad luck
   - Ⓑ good book
   - Ⓒ bad sport
   - Ⓓ good sport

4. **Which might you find in a *whimsical* story?**
   - Ⓕ a scientist who digs for dinosaur bones
   - Ⓖ a swimmer who is training for the Olympics
   - Ⓗ a friendly pink dragon that dances
   - Ⓙ a family that faces hardships as they travel in a covered wagon

Writing

If you could be talented in more than one area, what would you want your talents to be? Use **versatile** in your sentences.

_____

_____

_____

© Evan-Moor Corp. • EMC 2795 • A Word a Day

Week 8
A Word a Day

gratify

verb

to give pleasure or satisfaction

> Angela's good grades in school will **gratify** her parents.

Which words mean about the same as **gratify**?

- satisfy
- please
- annoy
- delight
- irritate

Describe something that **gratifies** you.

impartial

adjective

not favoring one over the other

synonym: fair

> It was hard for the referee to be **impartial** when his son's team was playing.

Complete this graphic organizer for **impartial**.

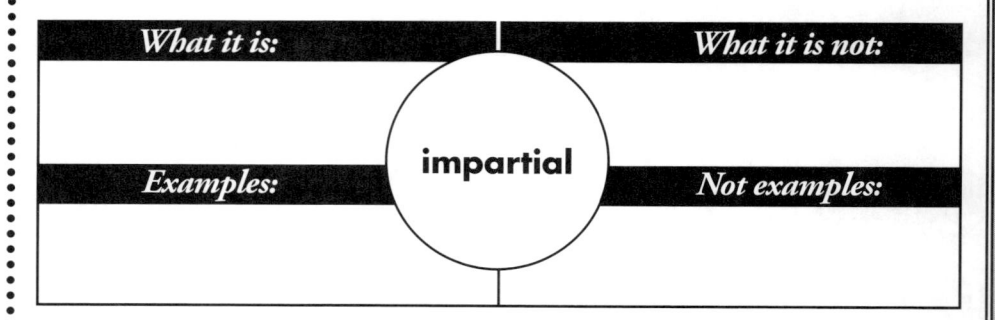

What it is:	What it is not:
Examples:	Not examples:

impartial

Why do you suppose it's important to have **impartial** judges?

Week 8
A Word a Day

knoll

noun

a small, rounded hill

> We climbed to the top of the **knoll** to get a clear view of the sunset.

In which of these places might you find a **knoll**?

- the country
- the ocean
- a golf course
- a tennis court
- a farm

Where can you find a **knoll** near your home?

tolerate

verb

to put up with something

synonym: endure

> When my dog could no longer **tolerate** the kitten's playful nibbling, he turned around and barked at her.

Which of these demonstrate the meaning of **tolerate**?

- I can't stand it when my big brother teases me!
- The patient put up with being in a cast for six months.
- Our teacher has no patience for those who say unkind things to their classmates.
- The mother waited patiently in line while her toddler tugged continuously on her sleeve.
- Pioneers suffered many hardships to settle the West.

Give an example of something you cannot **tolerate**.

Review

Week 8
A Word a Day

gratify • impartial • knoll • tolerate

Write on the board the four words studied this week. Read the words with the class and briefly review their meanings. Then conduct the oral activities below.

❶ Tell students that you are going to give them a clue about one of the words for the week. They are to find the word that answers the clue.

- This is how sports referees are supposed to be. **(impartial)**
- This word means about the same as *hill*. **(knoll)**
- You do this when you put up with a situation that isn't great. **(tolerate it)**
- You do this when you make someone happy. **(gratify that person)**

❷ Read each sentence and ask students to supply the correct word to complete the sentence.

- Dad will not ___ me ignoring my little brother. **(tolerate)**
- Contest judges must be as ___ as possible. **(impartial)**
- If I earn good grades this semester, it will ___ my parents. **(gratify)**
- The cottage sits on the ___ with a view down into the valley. **(knoll)**

❸ Read each sentence and ask students to tell which word is wrong. Then have them provide the correct word from the week's list.

- I can't forbid liars or thieves. **(forbid/tolerate)**
- From the top of this valley, you can see for miles. **(valley/knoll)**
- Referees must be unfair at all times. **(unfair/impartial)**
- My dog tries to displease me, but sometimes she misbehaves. **(displease/gratify)**

❹ Read each sentence and ask students to decide if it is true or false. If the sentence is false, instruct students to explain why.

- A knoll is taller than a mountain. **(false; a knoll is a low hill)**
- Few people will tolerate others' minor mistakes. **(false; most people will tolerate small mistakes)**
- It is part of a judge's job to remain impartial. **(true)**
- Not all people are gratified by the same things. **(true)**

Answers for page 35: 1. A, 2. G, 3. A, 4. F

34

A Word a Day • EMC 2795 • © Evan-Moor Corp.

Name _____

Week 8
A Word a Day

Review Words gratify • impartial • knoll • tolerate

Fill in the bubble next to the correct answer.

1. Which word is a synonym for *knoll*?
   Ⓐ hill
   Ⓑ valley
   Ⓒ river
   Ⓓ forest

2. Who should always be *impartial*?
   Ⓕ an art collector
   Ⓖ a courtroom judge
   Ⓗ a basketball fan
   Ⓙ a theatergoer

3. Which word is an antonym for *gratify*?
   Ⓐ displease
   Ⓑ miscommunicate
   Ⓒ dismantle
   Ⓓ misinterpret

4. In which sentence could *tolerate* be used to fill in the blank?
   Ⓕ I can't _____ really hot weather.
   Ⓖ I can't _____ that far without stopping.
   Ⓗ I can't _____ why I'm afraid of heights.
   Ⓙ I can't _____ asleep unless I read a book.

Writing

Write about one thing that you can tolerate and one thing that you can't tolerate. Use **tolerate** in your sentences.

_____

_____

_____

© Evan-Moor Corp. • EMC 2795 • A Word a Day

35

Week 9
A Word a Day

amateur

noun

a person who does something for pleasure, not for pay

If you excel in a sport as an **amateur**, you may be good enough to get paid to do it as a professional athlete.

Which word or words mean about the same as **amateur**?

- pro
- licensed expert
- nonprofessional
- unpaid
- hobbyist

What are some of the positive things about being an **amateur**?

rebellion

noun

a show of opposition to a form of authority

The Minutemen were an important part of the American colonials' **rebellion** against Britain.

Complete this graphic organizer for **rebellion**.

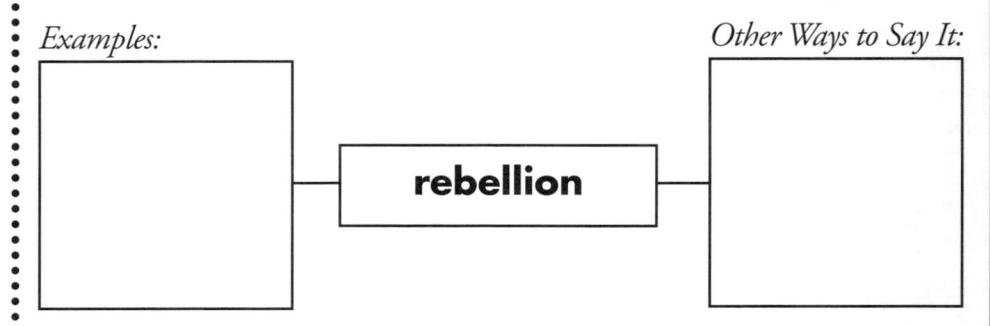

Examples: ☐ — **rebellion** — ☐ *Other Ways to Say It:*

What might be some of the reasons for people starting a **rebellion**?

Week 9
A Word a Day

appease

verb

to make calmer by giving in to demands

synonym: satisfy

> The band came back on stage and played another song to **appease** its screaming fans.

Which word or words mean about the same as **appease**?
- please
- calm down
- refuse
- soothe
- reject

Have your parents ever done anything to **appease** you? What were your demands, and how did you hope they would **appease** you?

partial

adjective

1. not complete
2. unfair favor to one side

> My teacher will not accept **partial** homework assignments, even from the students she seems to be **partial** to.

Which meaning is being described: "not complete" or "unfair favor"?
- Cindy let only her best friends play with her video games.
- I finished only half of my math homework.
- The music teacher assigned the solos to his favorite students.
- There is not enough information to complete the report.
- It seems like that skating judge gave the French skaters higher scores.

Can a coach be **partial** to one player over others? Do you think it's a good idea? Why or why not?

Review

Week 9
A Word a Day

amateur • rebellion • appease • partial

Write on the board the four words studied this week. Read the words with the class and briefly review their meanings. Then conduct the oral activities below.

❶ Tell students that you are going to give them a clue about one of the words for the week. They are to find the word that answers the clue.

- A referee should not be this way, even if he or she has a favorite team. **(partial to one team)**

- The American Revolution was one. **(a rebellion)**

- This word describes an athlete who doesn't get paid for playing a sport. **(amateur)**

- A nation's leaders do this when they give in to another nation's demands. **(appease that nation)**

❷ Read each sentence and ask students to supply the correct word to complete the sentence.

- Slaves had to ___ their owners for fear of stern punishment. **(appease)**

- Dylan performed as an ___ for many years before a theater company hired him. **(amateur)**

- Because the ___ succeeded, the king lost his kingdom. **(rebellion)**

- We can't play this game with a ___ deck of cards. **(partial)**

❸ Read each sentence and ask students to tell which word is wrong. Then have them provide the correct word from the week's list.

- A worker who doesn't upset his boss might lose his job. **(upset/appease)**

- Some plates and bowls broke, so we have only a complete set of dishes. **(complete/partial)**

- Many major league athletes played as professionals in high school and college. **(professionals/amateurs)**

- Peace broke out when the king placed a high tax on tea. **(Peace/Rebellion)**

❹ Read each sentence and ask students to decide if it is true or false. If the sentence is false, instruct students to explain why.

- Some rebellions turn into wars. **(true)**

- A dancer who is an amateur receives money for performing. **(false; he or she is unpaid)**

- It is legal for a courtroom judge to be partial to one side or the other. **(false; it is illegal)**

- *Appease* and *satisfy* are synonyms. **(true)**

Answers for page 39: 1. D, 2. G, 3. C, 4. F

Name _____

Week 9
A Word a Day

Review Words amateur • rebellion • appease • partial

Fill in the bubble next to the correct answer.

1. Which word is an antonym for *amateur*?
   - Ⓐ freshman
   - Ⓑ intellectual
   - Ⓒ apprentice
   - Ⓓ professional

2. Which word is not a synonym for *appease*?
   - Ⓕ soothe
   - Ⓖ displease
   - Ⓗ calm
   - Ⓙ satisfy

3. In which sentence is *partial* used correctly?
   - Ⓐ What a partial job you did on your project! Congratulations!
   - Ⓑ I love to brush my cat's partial coat of black-and-white fur.
   - Ⓒ The police found only a partial fingerprint at the crime scene.
   - Ⓓ The Pine family lives in a partial house with a swimming pool.

4. In which sentence could *rebellion* be used to fill in the blank?
   - Ⓕ The people started a ____ against their cruel king.
   - Ⓖ We held a festive ____ to honor our classroom aide.
   - Ⓗ A parents' group donated a new ____ to our school.
   - Ⓙ My mom attended her twentieth high school ____.

Writing

What sport or recreational activity would you like to participate in as an adult? Use **amateur** in your sentences.

_____

_____

© Evan-Moor Corp. • EMC 2795 • A Word a Day

Week 10
A Word a Day

falsehood

noun

a lie or an untruth

antonym: truth

Sheila's claim that she met a movie star when she visited Los Angeles turned out to be a **falsehood**. She merely saw a famous actor in a restaurant.

Complete this graphic organizer for **falsehood**.

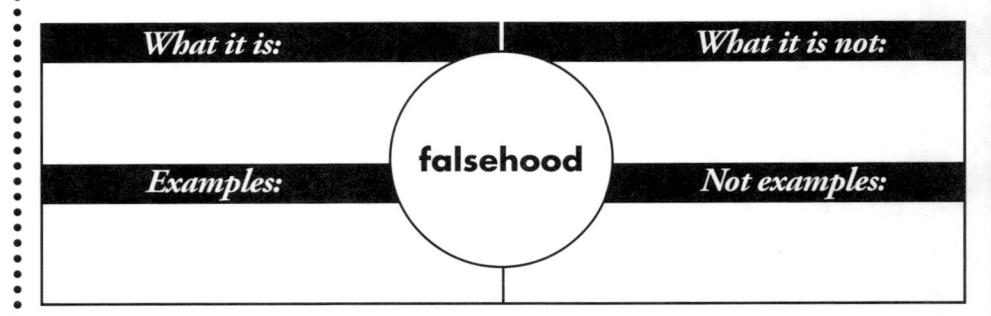

What it is:		*What it is not:*
Examples:	falsehood	*Not examples:*

Is it ever okay to tell a **falsehood**? Why or why not?

navigate

verb

to steer or direct the course of a ship or an aircraft

To **navigate** a ship in heavy fog is difficult because you can't see where the ship is headed.

Which of the following might help you to **navigate**?

- radar
- a map
- an anchor
- a compass
- a microphone

If you learned to **navigate**, would you prefer to **navigate** a ship or an airplane? Why?

Week 10
A Word a Day

kindling

noun

dried twigs or small pieces of wood used to start a fire

> The boys had to search the ground for **kindling** before they could build a campfire.

In which situations might **kindling** be used?

- baking cookies in an electric oven
- starting a fire in a wood-burning stove
- building a bonfire at the beach
- heating water in a microwave
- roasting marshmallows in a fireplace

Why do you need **kindling** to start a fire? Where could you find **kindling** near your home?

domestic

adjective

1. related to the home or family
2. tame; not wild

> Although I enjoy most **domestic** activities, I hate cleaning up after our **domestic** ferret.

Which meaning is being described: "related to the home" or "tame"?

- People have ridden horses for hundreds of years.
- Some birds are taught to say words.
- He likes to decorate his room with artwork.
- We depend on cows and goats to provide milk.
- Mom spent Saturday afternoon ironing shirts.

Name some of your **domestic** chores.

Review

Week 10
A Word a Day

falsehood • navigate • kindling • domestic

Write on the board the four words studied this week. Read the words with the class and briefly review their meanings. Then conduct the oral activities below.

1 Tell students that you are going to give them a clue about one of the words for the week. They are to find the word that answers the clue.

- People use this to start campfires. **(kindling)**
- You could use this word to describe chores that people do at home. **(domestic)**
- This is a lie. **(a falsehood)**
- Ships' captains use specialized instruments to do this. **(navigate their ships)**

2 Read each sentence and ask students to supply the correct word to complete the sentence.

- ____ catches fire more easily than thick pieces of firewood. **(Kindling)**
- Air traffic controllers help pilots to ____ planes into and out of airports. **(navigate)**
- Sometimes telling one ____ leads to telling more lies to cover up. **(falsehood)**
- Dad loves ____ activities such as cooking and gardening. **(domestic)**

3 Read each sentence and ask students to tell which word or words are wrong. Then have them provide the correct word from the week's list.

- A big log catches fire instantly. **(A big log/Kindling)**
- Cows are wild animals that live on farms. **(wild/domestic)**
- I hate it when people lie to me, so please don't tell me the truth. **(the truth/a falsehood)**

4 Read each sentence and ask students to decide if it is true or false. If the sentence is false, instruct students to explain why.

- Passengers are supposed to navigate ships. **(false; sailors steer and direct ships' courses)**
- Liars tell falsehoods. **(true)**
- Most wolves are domestic animals. **(false; most are wild)**
- Kindling catches fire easily because it is thin and dry. **(true)**

Answers for page 43: 1. D, 2. G, 3. A, 4. F

Name _____

Week 10
A Word a Day

Review Words falsehood • navigate • kindling • domestic

Fill in the bubble next to the correct answer.

1. Which of these animals is most likely to be *domestic*?
   - Ⓐ a wolf
   - Ⓑ a bear
   - Ⓒ a squirrel
   - Ⓓ a dog

2. Which word is a synonym for *navigate*?
   - Ⓕ exit
   - Ⓖ steer
   - Ⓗ build
   - Ⓙ board

3. Which phrase means the opposite of *falsehood*?
   - Ⓐ true statement
   - Ⓑ fantasy story
   - Ⓒ deliberate lie
   - Ⓓ traditional tale

4. In which sentence could *kindling* be used to fill in the blank?
   - Ⓕ We started a fire with newspaper and _____.
   - Ⓖ These antique chairs are made of oak _____.
   - Ⓗ There is a flower growing in that _____.
   - Ⓙ Each morning, I eat a bowl of milk and _____.

Writing

Write about your favorite domestic animal. Use **domestic** in your sentences.

_____

_____

_____

Week 11
A Word a Day

rustic

adjective

having to do with the countryside, not the city

> The **rustic** cabin looked out of place in the suburban neighborhood.

Which of these could be described as **rustic**?

- an apartment in a high-rise building
- a shopping mall
- a house made from logs
- a table made from unpolished planks of wood
- a wooden ceiling with open beams

What do you like about a **rustic** lifestyle? What do you like about city living?

lapse

noun

1. a small mistake or failure
2. the passing of time

> Forgive my **lapse** of good table manners, but it's been a two-year **lapse** since I've eaten in a fancy restaurant.

Which definition is being described: "a small mistake" or "the passing of time"?

- How have you been? I haven't seen you in months!
- I've had a lapse of memory; what's your name?
- The puppy can get its shots after a four-month lapse.
- I must have had a lapse of common sense to have bought that expensive evening gown.
- He broke his New Year's resolution after only a one-month lapse.

What is the **lapse** of time until your next birthday? What is the **lapse** of time before New Year's Day is here again?

Week 11
A Word a Day

correspond

verb

1. to communicate in writing
2. to match in some way

When you **correspond** with someone in Japan, you have to write the Japanese pictographs that **correspond** to that person's address.

Which of the following pairs **correspond**?

- the abbreviation "NY" and the state of Oregon
- the numeral 1 and the word "one"
- a red sock and a white sock
- a shoe and a glove
- the president of the United States and the prime minister of Canada

Do you **correspond** with anyone who lives far away? How do you prefer to **correspond**: by "snail mail" or by e-mail?

coy

adjective

shy or bashful

The **coy** child hid behind her mother when a stranger came to the door.

Complete this graphic organizer for **coy**.

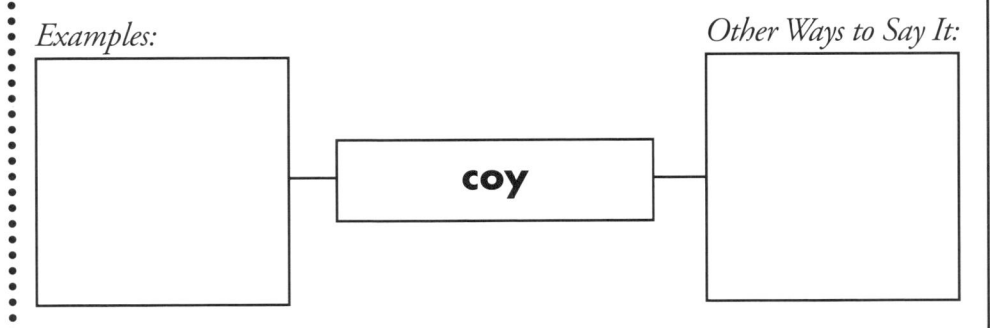

Examples: ▢ — **coy** — ▢ *Other Ways to Say It:*

How does a **coy** child act? How is it different from the way a **coy** adult might act?

Review

Week 11
A Word a Day

rustic • lapse • correspond • coy

Write on the board the four words studied this week. Read the words with the class and briefly review their meanings. Then conduct the oral activities below.

❶ Tell students that you are going to give them a clue about one of the words for the week. They are to find the word that answers the clue.

- This word describes the passage of time. **(lapse)**
- You might use this word to describe someone who avoids social situations. **(coy)**
- You might use this word to describe a farmhouse. **(rustic)**
- Pen pals do this. **(correspond)**

❷ Read each sentence and ask students to supply the correct word to complete the sentence.

- Does this sock ___ to one in the laundry basket, or have I lost one? **(correspond)**
- Since he hasn't seen me before, the baby is ___ with me. **(coy)**
- I had a ___ of good sense when I bought these ugly, expensive shoes. **(lapse)**
- Living in a log cabin with no electricity would be a little too ___ for me. **(rustic)**

❸ Read each sentence and ask students to tell which word or words are wrong. Then have them provide the correct word from the week's list.

- I moved to the country and soon got used to my new urban surroundings. **(urban/rustic)**
- Small children are often adventurous with unfamiliar people. **(adventurous/coy)**
- The word *nine* and the numeral 9 are totally different. **(are totally different/correspond)**

❹ Read each sentence and ask students to decide if it is true or false. If the sentence is false, instruct students to explain why.

- If you have a lapse in judgment, you might do something you shouldn't. **(true)**
- Skyscrapers look rustic. **(false; they look as though they belong in big cities)**
- Most coy people don't talk much at parties. **(true)**
- The Spanish word *sí* corresponds to the English word *yes*. **(true)**

Answers for page 47: 1. D, 2. H, 3. C, 4. J

46   A Word a Day • EMC 2795 • Evan-Moor Corp.

Name _____

Week 11
A Word a Day

Review Words   rustic • lapse • correspond • coy

Fill in the bubble next to the correct answer.

1. **When friends *correspond* with each other, which of these do they do?**
   - Ⓐ They attend school together.
   - Ⓑ They spend weekends together.
   - Ⓒ They talk on the phone together.
   - Ⓓ They exchange letters or e-mails.

2. **Which word is a synonym for *rustic*?**
   - Ⓕ snobbish
   - Ⓖ upscale
   - Ⓗ rural
   - Ⓙ casual

3. **Which word is an antonym for *coy*?**
   - Ⓐ quiet
   - Ⓑ plump
   - Ⓒ bold
   - Ⓓ obvious

4. **In which sentence could *lapse* be used to fill in the blank?**
   - Ⓕ After school, I love to ____ with friends.
   - Ⓖ Just ____ back in this comfy chair and relax.
   - Ⓗ Next year, we plan to ____ to California.
   - Ⓙ After a ____ of six months, the neglected plants had died.

Writing

Write about how country life is different from city life. Use **rustic** in your sentences.

_____
_____
_____

© Evan-Moor Corp. • EMC 2795 • A Word a Day

47

Week 12
A Word a Day

ancestor

noun

a member of your family who lived a long time ago, even before your grandparents

I have an **ancestor** who fought in the American Civil War.

Which of these are **ancestors**?
- your second cousin
- a family member who lived 150 years ago
- the grandson of your younger brother
- a relative who died in 1825
- your grandfather's great-grandfather

What do you know about your **ancestors**? Who is one of your most interesting **ancestors**?

dimension

noun

a measurement of length, width, or thickness

We need to figure out the room's **dimensions** so we can buy the right amount of paint.

Why might you want to find the **dimensions** of something?
- to find a box to ship it in
- to know if you can move it through a doorway
- to decide if you like it
- to see if you can lift it
- to know if you can put it in the car

Choose an object in your classroom and guess what its **dimensions** might be. Use a ruler or yardstick to see how close your estimate was to the actual **dimensions**.

Week 12
A Word a Day

dominate

verb

to rule or control by strength or power

The king used his soldiers to help him **dominate** the kingdom.

Complete this graphic organizer for **dominate**.

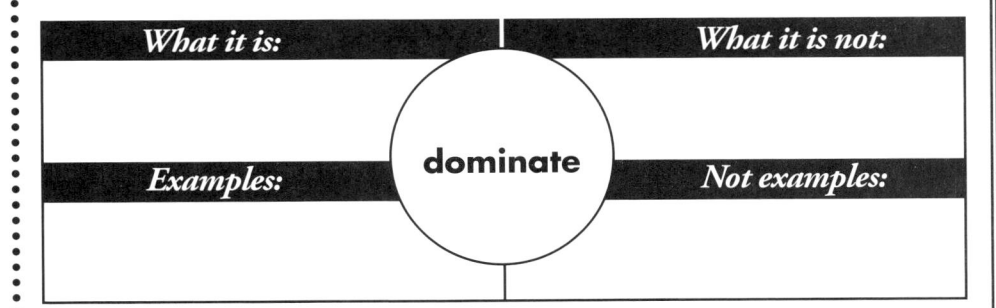

What it is:	What it is not:
Examples:	Not examples:

(dominate)

Has someone ever tried to **dominate** you? How did you feel? Have you ever tried to **dominate** someone? Why?

invincible

adjective

not able to be defeated

With five victories and no defeats, our team has been **invincible** this season.

Which of these characters are **invincible**?

- Little Red Riding Hood
- John Henry
- Little Boy Blue
- Spiderman
- Batman

Do you think there is anyone in real life who is **invincible**? Explain your answer.

Review

Week 12
A Word a Day

ancestor • dimension • dominate • invincible

Write on the board the four words studied this week. Read the words with the class and briefly review their meanings. Then conduct the oral activities below.

1 Tell students that you are going to give them a clue about one of the words for the week. They are to find the word that answers the clue.

- Unfair rulers do this. (**dominate their people**)
- This is a family member who lived long ago. (**an ancestor**)
- This is an object's length, width, or thickness. (**a dimension**)
- You might use this word to describe a superhero. (**invincible**)

2 Read each sentence and ask students to supply the correct word to complete the sentence.

- In movies, villains use ruthless methods to ___ people. (**dominate**)
- Taylor says that her ___ was a Spanish explorer who lived in the 1700s. (**ancestor**)
- Let's measure the refrigerator to find its ___. (**dimensions**)
- The ancient Roman army seemed ___, but Rome eventually lost its power. (**invincible**)

3 Read each sentence and ask students to tell which word or words are wrong. Then have them provide the correct word from the week's list.

- Our undefeated team will surely lose to the Tigers. (**lose to/dominate**)
- A grandson of mine immigrated to the United States in the 1800s. (**A grandson/An ancestor**)
- No one can beat Max at chess—he's a terrible player! (**a terrible player/invincible**)
- Use this tape measure to find the weight of the table. (**weight/dimensions**)

4 Read each sentence and ask students to decide if it is true or false. If the sentence is false, instruct students to explain why.

- Color is a dimension. (**false; a dimension is a measurement**)
- The U.S. president has the right to dominate everyone else in government. (**false; he or she must share power with other leaders such as senators**)
- Your great-grandma's great-grandma was an ancestor of yours. (**true**)
- *Invincible* and *beatable* are antonyms. (**true**)

Answers for page 51: 1. C, 2. J, 3. B, 4. F

50

A Word a Day • EMC 2795 • © Evan-Moor Corp.

Name _____

Week 12
A Word a Day

Review Words ancestor • dimension • dominate • invincible

Fill in the bubble next to the correct answer.

1. Which of these is not a *dimension*?
   - Ⓐ length
   - Ⓑ width
   - Ⓒ weight
   - Ⓓ thickness

2. Which word is a synonym for *dominate*?
   - Ⓕ ignore
   - Ⓖ befriend
   - Ⓗ teach
   - Ⓙ rule

3. Which is true of an *invincible* army?
   - Ⓐ It has never won a battle.
   - Ⓑ Other armies cannot defeat it.
   - Ⓒ An enemy army has just defeated it.
   - Ⓓ Its general is a weak leader.

4. In which sentence could *ancestor* be used to fill in the blank?
   - Ⓕ In 1849, my family's ____ searched for gold in California.
   - Ⓖ Someday, an ____ of mine may invent a nonpolluting fuel.
   - Ⓗ My little ____ goes to the same preschool that I attended.
   - Ⓙ My mom's ____ lives a few blocks from our house.

Writing

Write an interesting fact about your family's ancestors. Use **ancestor** or **ancestors** in your sentences.

_____
_____
_____

© Evan-Moor Corp. • EMC 2795 • A Word a Day

Week 13
A Word a Day

muse

verb

to think deeply

> My mother had to **muse** for a while before deciding to let me have a slumber party.

Which words mean about the same as **muse**?

- consider
- ponder
- forget
- reflect on
- ask

What is a decision you have had to **muse** about? Give an example of something you had to **muse** about recently.

paraphrase

verb

to use other words to explain something

> The teacher asked us to **paraphrase** the story in fifty words or less.

Complete this graphic organizer for **paraphrase**.

Examples: *Other Ways to Say It:*

[ ] —— [paraphrase] —— [ ]

Do you prefer to hear someone **paraphrase** an exciting story, or would you rather hear the whole thing? Why?

Week 13
A Word a Day

vulnerable
adjective

capable of being harmed or injured

Without its mother, the baby bird was **vulnerable** on the ground.

Which of these animals are **vulnerable**?
- a dog sitting by a warm fireplace
- an orphaned cheetah cub
- a lion alone on the plain
- a kitten on a busy street
- a dog lost outside

Would you feel **vulnerable** if you had to sleep outdoors without a tent? What other situations might make you feel **vulnerable**?

tariff
noun

a tax paid on products that are imported or exported

On December 16, 1773, 150 American colonists dressed as Mohawk Indians dumped 342 crates of tea into Boston Harbor to protest a British **tariff** on tea.

Which items might have a **tariff** placed on them?
- a German car bought in the United States
- American apples bought in Costa Rica
- a cowboy hat made and sold in Texas
- food from your garden
- a rug made in India

What is something that your family has bought that probably included a **tariff** in the price?

Review

Week 13
A Word a Day

muse • paraphrase • vulnerable • tariff

Write on the board the four words studied this week. Read the words with the class and briefly review their meanings. Then conduct the oral activities below.

❶ Tell students that you are going to give them a clue about one of the words for the week. They are to find the word that answers the clue.

- You use your own words to do this. **(paraphrase)**
- You might do this when you have something important to think over. **(muse)**
- If a company brings foreign products into the United States, it may have to pay one. **(a tariff)**
- This word describes an unprotected creature. **(vulnerable)**

❷ Read each sentence and ask students to supply the correct word to complete the sentence.

- If you are run-down and tired, you are more ____ to illness. **(vulnerable)**
- The principal had to ____ about how to punish the students who broke the rules. **(muse)**
- I can't remember her exact words, so I'll have to ____ what she said. **(paraphrase)**
- The department store had to pay a ____ on a shipment of clothing from India. **(tariff)**

❸ Read each list of words and phrases. Ask students to supply the word that fits best with each.

- unprotected, weak, open to attack **(vulnerable)**
- restate, rephrase, sum up in your own words **(paraphrase)**
- ponder, consider, think over **(muse)**
- import tax, export tax **(tariff)**

❹ Read each sentence and ask students to decide if it is true or false. If the sentence is false, instruct students to explain why.

- An antelope is more vulnerable if it becomes separated from its herd. **(true)**
- You pay a tariff when you buy food grown on local farms. **(false; a tariff is an import or export tax)**
- Paraphrasing what someone said is the same as quoting him or her. **(false; you use your own words to paraphrase)**
- *Muse* and *ponder* are synonyms. **(true)**

Answers for page 55: 1. D, 2. G, 3. C, 4. H

Week 13
A Word a Day

Name _____

Review Words muse • paraphrase • vulnerable • tariff

Fill in the bubble next to the correct answer.

1. **Which type of tax is a *tariff*?**
   - Ⓐ a tax on workers' wages
   - Ⓑ a tax on people's homes
   - Ⓒ a tax that hotel guests pay
   - Ⓓ a tax on imports or exports

2. **Which word is a synonym for *muse*?**
   - Ⓕ slide
   - Ⓖ ponder
   - Ⓗ float
   - Ⓙ dance

3. **Which word is an antonym for *vulnerable*?**
   - Ⓐ intolerable
   - Ⓑ invisible
   - Ⓒ invincible
   - Ⓓ insufficient

4. **In which sentence could *paraphrase* be used to fill in the blank?**
   - Ⓕ I can ____ Mark's exact words. He said, "It'll be great to see you."
   - Ⓖ She asked for a quick response, so let's ____ Marcy right now.
   - Ⓗ I can't give you an exact quote, but I can ____ what Matt said.
   - Ⓙ Newspaper interviewers try to ____ exactly what people say.

Writing

Write about the actions you would take when riding a bicycle so you aren't vulnerable to injury. Use **vulnerable** in your sentences.

_____

_____

_____

Week 14
A Word a Day

urge

verb

to speak or argue strongly in favor of

noun

a strong desire

The basketball coach had to **urge** her star player to control the **urge** to take wild shots.

Which meaning is being used: "to speak in favor of" or "a strong desire"?

- Our doctor urged us to eat more vegetables.
- Max had to fight the urge to take a fourth piece of cake.
- I strongly urge you to start studying for next Friday's test.
- I had to resist the urge to open my birthday presents a day early.
- We were urged to use more than one source for our research paper.

What would you say or do to **urge** your family to recycle?

tactful

adjective

thoughtful and sensitive in dealing with others

The **tactful** waiter quickly and quietly removed the glass of water with a fly in it.

Which of these are examples of **tactful** statements?

- Turn down that music right now!
- Do you think you could use your earphones to listen to your music?
- I think you could improve your story if you described the main character in more detail.
- Your story is really boring.
- This new hairstyle is attractive on you.

Give some other examples of ways to behave in a **tactful** manner. What are some examples of not behaving in a **tactful** manner?

Week 14
A Word a Day

belfry

noun

a tower where bells are hung

The bell ringer climbed the winding staircase to the **belfry** every evening at 5:00 to ring the hour.

Which of the following might you see in a **belfry**?

- coins
- stairs
- a bell
- a train
- a rope

Is there a **belfry** in our town? If not, have you seen a **belfry**? Where?

critique

verb

to give an opinion of the positive and negative points of something

Before I write my final story draft, I will ask some classmates to **critique** my rough draft to get ideas for ways to improve the plot.

Complete this graphic organizer for **critique**.

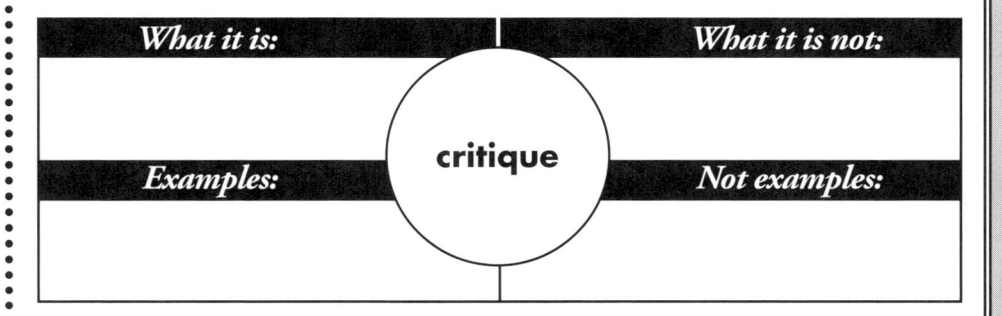

What it is:	What it is not:
Examples:	Not examples:

(center: critique)

Why might it be difficult to **critique** your own work? Do you think it would be easy or difficult to **critique** your best friend's work?

Review

Week 14
A Word a Day

urge • tactful • belfry • critique

Write on the board the four words studied this week. Read the words with the class and briefly review their meanings. Then conduct the oral activities below.

❶ Tell students that you are going to give them a clue about one of the words for the week. They are to find the word that answers the clue.

- You evaluate someone's work when you do this. **(critique it)**
- There might be one on top of a church. **(a belfry)**
- It might be hard to resist something if you have one of these. **(an urge)**
- This word describes someone who avoids hurting people's feelings. **(tactful)**

❷ Read each sentence and ask students to supply the correct word to complete the sentence.

- Please ____ my story so I can use your comments to rewrite it. **(critique)**
- The old-fashioned schoolhouse has a ____ with a large iron bell. **(belfry)**
- I ____ you to put off your trip until the storm is over. **(urge)**
- I don't mind having my scout leader critique my projects, because he is always ____. **(tactful)**

❸ Read each list of words and phrases. Ask students to supply the word that fits best with each.

- church, schoolhouse, bell tower **(belfry)**
- thoughtful, sensitive, careful of others' feelings **(tactful)**
- desire, impulse, irresistible **(urge)**
- offer feedback, criticize, analyze, praise **(critique)**

❹ Read each sentence and ask students to decide if it is true or false. If the sentence is false, instruct students to explain why.

- Few modern buildings have belfries. **(true)**
- It is tactful to tell someone that he or she needs to lose weight. **(false; it's insensitive to the person's feelings)**
- It is a teacher's job to critique student work. **(true)**
- Parents usually urge their kids to have sleepovers on school nights. **(false; parents usually forbid their kids to do that)**

Answers for page 59: 1. C, 2. J, 3. A, 4. F

Name _____

Week 14
A Word a Day

Review Words   urge • tactful • belfry • critique

Fill in the bubble next to the correct answer.

1. **Which of the following gets paid to *critique* movies?**
   - Ⓐ the audience
   - Ⓑ the director
   - Ⓒ a movie critic
   - Ⓓ a movie theater usher

2. **Which word or phrase has the same meaning as *belfry*?**
   - Ⓕ belle of the ball
   - Ⓖ dinner bell
   - Ⓗ cowbell
   - Ⓙ bell tower

3. **Which word is an antonym for *tactful*?**
   - Ⓐ insensitive
   - Ⓑ inefficient
   - Ⓒ insurmountable
   - Ⓓ inexpressible

4. **In which sentence could *urge* be used to fill in the blank?**
   - Ⓕ I ____ you to eat healthy snacks and get plenty of exercise.
   - Ⓖ Let's ____ Brenda for the great job she did in the school play.
   - Ⓗ When my dog follows my commands, I ____ her with a treat.
   - Ⓙ We wish to ____ you so very much for your kind hospitality.

Writing

How could you tell a classmate in a tactful way that she has food on her face? Use **tactful** in your sentences.

_____

_____

_____

Week 15
A Word a Day

humble

adjective

1. not proud; modest
2. simple; not fancy

The **humble** artist refused to take large sums of money for his beautiful paintings. He lived simply in a **humble** studio outside the city.

Which meaning is being described: "not proud" or "not fancy"?

- The college student lived in a very small apartment.
- The actor did not think he deserved the award for "best performance in a play."
- In his first job, the billionaire worked as a humble dishwasher.
- Eliona was embarrassed by the many compliments she received on her speech.
- The camp food was plain, but it was delicious and filling.

Describe something or someone you know to be **humble**.

friction

noun

disagreement between people or groups of people

There was **friction** between the two teams when a wild pitch injured the batter.

Which words mean about the same as **friction**?

- anger
- conflict
- friendship
- peace
- hostility

Has there ever been **friction** on the playground? What caused it? How was it resolved?

Week 15
A Word a Day

loathe

verb

to dislike greatly

antonym: adore

I **loathe** running around the track after it rains, because I always get covered with mud.

Which words mean about the same as **loathe**?

- appreciate
- despise
- admire
- detest
- hate

What is something you **loathe**? Do you ever **loathe** something that is actually good for you? If so, give an example.

sincere

adjective

genuine; true

Cory's **sincere** apology made me feel better because I could tell he was truly sorry.

Complete this graphic organizer for **sincere**.

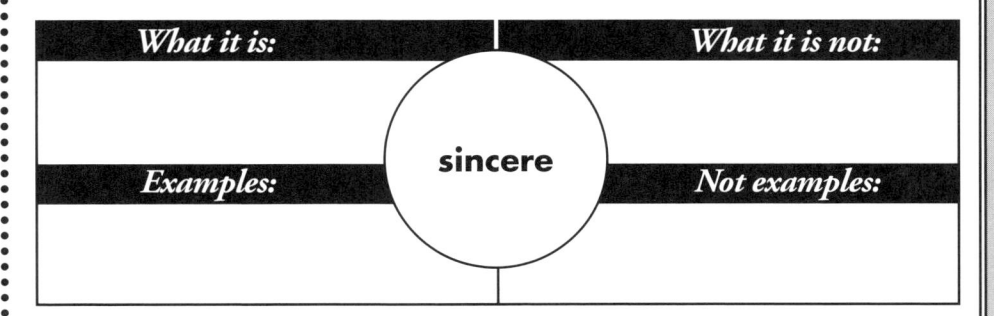

What it is:	What it is not:
Examples:	**Not examples:**

(with **sincere** in a center circle)

How do you know if someone is being **sincere** or not? How does it feel when someone is not **sincere** with you? Are you always **sincere**?

Review

Week 15
A Word a Day

humble • friction • loathe • sincere

Write on the board the four words studied this week. Read the words with the class and briefly review their meanings. Then conduct the oral activities below.

❶ Tell students that you are going to give them a clue about one of the words for the week. They are to find the word that answers the clue.

- Two people who are arguing are experiencing this. **(friction)**
- This is a synonym for *detest*. **(loathe)**
- This word describes someone who is not overly proud of themselves. **(humble)**
- This word describes someone who means what he or she says. **(sincere)**

❷ Read each sentence and ask students to supply the correct word to complete the sentence.

- I ____ cooked raisins because of their disgusting texture. **(loathe)**
- From the serious look on his face, I could tell that Danny's apology was ____. **(sincere)**
- In the folk tale, the old couple lived in a ____ little hut made from mud and straw. **(humble)**
- The ____ between the two women made the dinner party unpleasant. **(friction)**

❸ Read each sentence and ask students to tell which word is wrong. Then have them provide the correct word from the week's list.

- Molly is so conceited that praise makes her feel uncomfortable. **(conceited/humble)**
- Dylan's phony smile makes me feel better. **(phony/sincere)**
- I love taking out the trash because the smell makes me sick. **(love/loathe)**
- The mood of the team was tense because of the agreement between the two best players. **(agreement/friction)**

❹ Read each sentence and ask students to decide if it is true or false. If the sentence is false, instruct students to explain why.

- Most people loathe disgusting odors. **(true)**
- You cannot always tell whether someone is sincere. **(true)**
- If there is friction in the classroom, we will all feel at peace. **(false; we will feel tense and uneasy)**
- Most movie stars live in humble homes. **(false; most live in fancy homes)**

Answers for page 63: 1. C, 2. H, 3. D, 4. F

Name _____

Week 15
A Word a Day

Review Words humble • friction • loathe • sincere

Fill in the bubble next to the correct answer.

1. **Which action is not likely to reduce *friction* between people?**
   - Ⓐ talking it out
   - Ⓑ making a compromise
   - Ⓒ having a fight
   - Ⓓ agreeing to disagree

2. **Which word is an antonym for *sincere*?**
   - Ⓕ grouchy
   - Ⓖ unattractive
   - Ⓗ phony
   - Ⓙ unkind

3. **Which word is an antonym for *loathe*?**
   - Ⓐ excuse
   - Ⓑ remember
   - Ⓒ reject
   - Ⓓ adore

4. **A *humble* person would be most likely to say which of the following?**
   - Ⓕ "I'm not worthy of this honor."
   - Ⓖ "Thanks for recognizing my superior skills."
   - Ⓗ "I truly deserve to be president."
   - Ⓙ "You were very smart to hire me."

Writing

Write about a food or beverage that you loathe. Explain why it disgusts you. Use **loathe** in your sentences.

_____

_____

_____

© Evan-Moor Corp. • EMC 2795 • A Word a Day

Week 16
A Word a Day

tragedy

noun

1. an unfortunate or sad event
2. a play, movie, or story with a terribly sad ending

The sinking of the ocean liner *Titanic* was a terrible **tragedy**. It cost millions of dollars to film the **tragedy** *Titanic*, which was a huge hit.

Which of these are examples of a **tragedy**?
- The play ended with singing and dancing.
- There wasn't a dry eye in the theater when the hero died.
- Thousands were left homeless following the flood.
- The wedding was a joyful event.
- The book was about an orphan who lost both parents in an airplane crash.

Tell the plot of a **tragedy** that you've read, seen as a play, or seen at the movies.

pulsate

verb

to beat in rhythm, as the heart does

On foggy nights, you can see the glow of the roller coaster's flashing neon lights **pulsate** through the mist.

Which words mean about the same as **pulsate**?
- flutter
- throb
- flicker
- thump
- pound

Besides a heart and lights, what other things **pulsate**?

Week 16
A Word a Day

undaunted

adjective

not discouraged; not hesitating because of danger or difficulties

The hiker's hopes for rescue remained **undaunted**, even though he had been lost in the wilderness for two days.

Which words mean about the same as **undaunted**?
- unafraid
- fearless
- terrified
- steadfast
- optimistic

Give an example of someone who was **undaunted**. Have you ever been **undaunted**? Describe the situation.

aptitude

noun

a natural ability or talent

Lucita has an excellent sense of color and shows a strong **aptitude** for painting.

Complete this graphic organizer for **aptitude**.

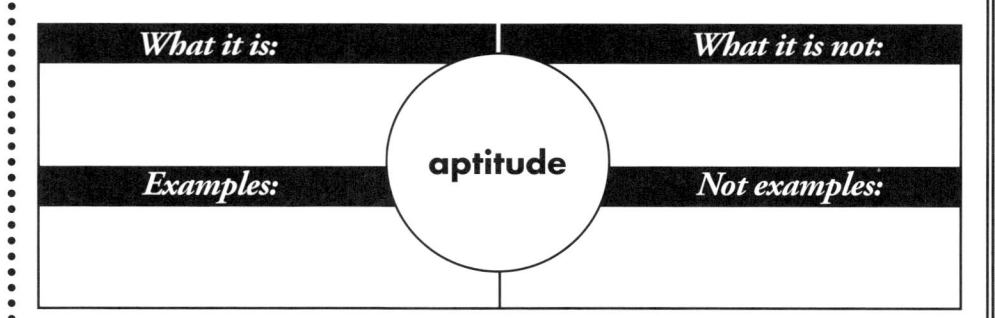

What it is:	What it is not:
Examples:	Not examples:

(center: aptitude)

Have you discovered something for which you have an **aptitude**? Tell the class about it.

Review

Week 16
A Word a Day

tragedy • pulsate • undaunted • aptitude

Write on the board the four words studied this week. Read the words with the class and briefly review their meanings. Then conduct the oral activities below.

1 Tell students that you are going to give them a clue about one of the words for the week. They are to find the word that answers the clue.

- Your blood does this in your arteries. **(pulsates)**
- A fatal car crash is one. **(a tragedy)**
- It's easier to excel at a sport if you have this. **(an aptitude for it)**
- When you face a major disappointment, it can be hard to remain this way. **(undaunted)**

2 Read each sentence and ask students to supply the correct word to complete the sentence.

- Despite his difficulties, our hero remained ___. **(undaunted)**
- Lily shows a strong ___ for math. She hopes to be a math major in college. **(aptitude)**
- Drumbeats ___ through the whole house when my brother plays a CD. **(pulsate)**
- *Romeo and Juliet* is a famous ___ by Shakespeare in which both Romeo and Juliet die. **(tragedy)**

3 Read each list of words and phrases. Ask students to supply the word that fits best with each.

- unafraid, courageous, fearless, not discouraged **(undaunted)**
- heartbeat, drumbeat, rhythmic throbbing **(pulsate)**
- car accident, natural disaster, accidental death **(tragedy)**
- natural talent, ability, gift **(aptitude)**

4 Read each sentence and ask students to decide if it is true or false. If the sentence is false, instruct students to explain why.

- Most children's movies are tragedies. **(false; most have happy endings)**
- In most fairy tales, heroes remain undaunted. **(true)**
- Deaf people can feel the pulsating of music. **(true)**
- An aptitude is similar to a mental block. **(false; an aptitude helps one to be good at something, whereas a mental block restricts action)**

Answers for page 67: 1. C, 2. G, 3. A, 4. G

Name _____

Week 16
A Word a Day

Review Words   tragedy • pulsate • undaunted • aptitude

Fill in the bubble next to the correct answer.

1. Which of these *pulsates*?
   - Ⓐ your fingernails
   - Ⓑ your hair
   - Ⓒ your heart
   - Ⓓ your clothing

2. Which word is an antonym for *tragedy*?
   - Ⓕ fact
   - Ⓖ comedy
   - Ⓗ drama
   - Ⓙ falsehood

3. Which word is an antonym for *undaunted*?
   - Ⓐ discouraged
   - Ⓑ cheerful
   - Ⓒ obedient
   - Ⓓ calm

4. Who is most likely to have an *aptitude* for art?
   - Ⓕ an art store owner
   - Ⓖ someone with artistic talent
   - Ⓗ someone who paints by numbers
   - Ⓙ someone who isn't interested in art

Writing

Write about a time when you were undaunted, even though you faced obstacles. Use **undaunted** in your sentences.

_____

_____

_____

© Evan-Moor Corp. • EMC 2795 • A Word a Day

Week 17
A Word a Day

balmy

adjective

soothing and mild

The **balmy** spring weather felt refreshing after the long winter.

Which words mean about the same as **balmy**?
- fair
- cold
- warm
- harsh
- gentle

Describe a **balmy** spring day or a **balmy** tropical night.

bask

verb

to lie in and enjoy a warm place

On warm spring days, my cat loves to sit on the windowsill and **bask** in the sun.

Complete this graphic organizer for **bask**.

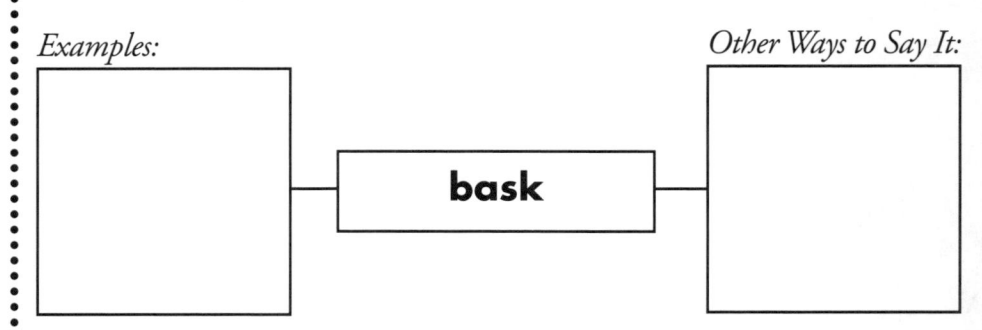

Examples: — **bask** — *Other Ways to Say It:*

Besides cats, what other animals **bask** in the sun?
Why isn't it a good idea for humans to **bask** in the sun for long periods of time?

Week 17
A Word a Day

denominator

noun

the number below the line in a fraction

In a fraction, the **denominator** indicates the number of parts a whole number is divided into.

Which of these fractions is equivalent to one that has a **denominator** of 8 and a numerator of 4?

- ¼
- ¾
- ½
- ³⁄₆
- ⁴⁄₈

If you were dividing a pizza into ten slices, what number would be in the **denominator** of the fraction that shows one slice of pizza?

vertical

adjective

straight up and down

The first hill on the roller coaster ride was nearly **vertical**.

Which words or phrases mean about the same as **vertical**?

- horizontal
- perpendicular to the ground
- upright
- flat
- level

Name some things in the classroom that are **vertical**.

Review

Week 17
A Word a Day

balmy • bask • denominator • vertical

Write on the board the four words studied this week. Read the words with the class and briefly review their meanings. Then conduct the oral activities below.

❶ Tell students that you are going to give them a clue about one of the words for the week. They are to find the word that answers the clue.

- You might use this word to describe a skyscraper's walls. **(vertical)**
- In a fraction, this is the number that is not the numerator. **(the denominator)**
- This word describes what you do when you experience and enjoy warmth. **(bask)**
- This word describes a kind of weather that most people like. **(balmy)**

❷ Read each sentence and ask students to supply the correct word to complete the sentence.

- The ___ in the fraction 3/4 tells that one whole is divided into four parts. **(denominator)**
- You print a lowercase *L* by making a ___ line. **(vertical)**
- In Hawaii, countless vacationers lie on beaches and ___ in the sun. **(bask)**
- People from colder, harsher climates appreciate Hawaii's ___ breezes. **(balmy)**

❸ Read each sentence and ask students to tell which word is wrong. Then have them provide the correct word from the week's list.

- In the fraction 7/8, the numeral 8 is the numerator. **(numerator/denominator)**
- The lone soldier's upright figure made a horizontal line against the sky. **(horizontal/vertical)**
- On this peaceful tropical island, visitors enjoy hurricane-force breezes. **(hurricane-force/balmy)**

❹ Read each sentence and ask students to decide if it is true or false. If the sentence is false, instruct students to explain why.

- A reptile basks in the sun to raise its body temperature. **(true)**
- Most people enjoy sitting outdoors on balmy days. **(true)**
- A printed *W* has vertical lines in it. **(false; it has diagonal lines)**
- In the fraction 4/5, the numeral 4 is the denominator. **(false; the numeral 5 is the denominator)**

Answers for page 71: 1. C, 2. G, 3. B, 4. H

Name _____

Week 17
A Word a Day

Review Words balmy • bask • denominator • vertical

Fill in the bubble next to the correct answer.

1. In which of these fractions is 3 the *denominator*?
   Ⓐ 3/5
   Ⓑ 3/4
   Ⓒ 1/3
   Ⓓ 4/5

2. Which word is an antonym for *vertical*?
   Ⓕ slender
   Ⓖ horizontal
   Ⓗ tall
   Ⓙ diagonal

3. Which is a *balmy* day?
   Ⓐ a tragic day
   Ⓑ a warm day
   Ⓒ a snowy day
   Ⓓ a holiday

4. Where are people most likely to *bask* in the sun?
   Ⓕ at school
   Ⓖ in the ocean
   Ⓗ on beaches
   Ⓙ in their cars

Writing

Write about what you like to do outside when the weather is balmy. Use **balmy** in your sentences.

_____

_____

_____

© Evan-Moor Corp. • EMC 2795 • A Word a Day   **71**

Week 18
A Word a Day

ovation

noun

a loud and enthusiastic show of approval

The audience gave the choir a standing **ovation** at the end of the concert.

In which of these places might you give an **ovation**?

- the box office
- a skating competition
- a football game
- a piano recital
- a taxicab

When was the last time you gave an **ovation**?

emancipate

verb

to set free from slavery or control

President Lincoln helped to **emancipate** the slaves in the South.

Complete this graphic organizer for **emancipate**.

Examples: — **emancipate** — *Other Ways to Say It:*

Besides slavery, from what other circumstances might people struggle to **emancipate** themselves?

Week 18
A Word a Day

susceptible

adjective

easily influenced or affected

> The medical assistant wore a surgical mask so she wouldn't be **susceptible** to catching colds.

Which words mean about the same as **susceptible**?

- unprotected
- vulnerable
- sensitive
- secure
- safe

If it's easy to convince someone to do what you want, that person is **susceptible** to being persuaded. In what situation might it be good to be **susceptible**? In what situation might it be bad to be **susceptible**?

tarnish

verb

to dull the shine of a metal surface by exposure to air

> If left on the table, the silver candlesticks will **tarnish** and require polishing.

Which of these items could **tarnish**?

- a wooden bowl on a shelf
- a brass teakettle on the stove
- a glass vase on a wooden table
- a sterling silver necklace
- Grandmother's fine silverware in its velvet case

Is there anything in the classroom that can **tarnish**? What about in your home?

Review

Week 18
A Word a Day

ovation • emancipate • susceptible • tarnish

Write on the board the four words studied this week. Read the words with the class and briefly review their meanings. Then conduct the oral activities below.

❶ Tell students that you are going to give them a clue about one of the words for the week. They are to find the word that answers the clue.

- This word describes someone who could easily catch a certain disease. **(susceptible)**

- Silver platters sometimes do this. **(tarnish)**

- Actors often receive one at the end of a hit play. **(an ovation)**

- This word describes what a person does when he or she releases control of another person. **(emancipates him or her)**

❷ Read each sentence and ask students to supply the correct word to complete the sentence.

- Sterling silver spoons ____. You must polish them regularly. **(tarnish)**

- Slave owners who thought that slavery was wrong decided to ____ their slaves. **(emancipate)**

- Any performer loves to receive a standing ____. **(ovation)**

- Great-Grandpa Rex is ____ to bronchitis whenever he gets a cold. **(susceptible)**

❸ Read each sentence and ask students to tell which word or words are wrong. Then have them provide the correct word from the week's list.

- Since Amy is immune to winter colds, she needs to get plenty of rest. **(immune/susceptible)**

- If you don't pack it away in its box, your silverware will grow shiny. **(grow shiny/tarnish)**

- President Lincoln decided to imprison slaves during the Civil War. **(imprison/emancipate)**

❹ Read each sentence and ask students to decide if it is true or false. If the sentence is false, instruct students to explain why.

- Metal looks dull or discolored when it tarnishes. **(true)**

- A good diet can make you less susceptible to illness. **(true)**

- A standing ovation means that the audience loved the performance. **(true)**

- President Lincoln emancipated the slaves in 2000. **(false; he did so in the 1860s)**

Answers for page 75: 1. B, 2. J, 3. C, 4. J

Week 18
A Word a Day

Name _____

Review Words: ovation • emancipate • susceptible • tarnish

Fill in the bubble next to the correct answer.

1. Which material can *tarnish*?
   - Ⓐ brick
   - Ⓑ metal
   - Ⓒ plastic
   - Ⓓ wood

2. Which word is an antonym for *emancipate*?
   - Ⓕ rescue
   - Ⓖ confuse
   - Ⓗ protect
   - Ⓙ enslave

3. Who is most likely to receive an *ovation*?
   - Ⓐ a bank teller
   - Ⓑ a store clerk
   - Ⓒ a performer
   - Ⓓ a carpenter

4. In which sentence is *susceptible* used correctly?
   - Ⓕ Yummy, what a susceptible meal Mom made last night!
   - Ⓖ My dog is very susceptible to tennis balls, bones, and squirrels.
   - Ⓗ I wish I could stop humming that susceptible tune, but I can't.
   - Ⓙ Lack of sleep can make people more susceptible to illness.

Writing

Write about a performer you know or have heard of. Use **ovation** in your sentences.

_____

_____

Week 19
A Word a Day

pell-mell

adjective

in a hasty, confused, and disorderly manner

The books were thrown **pell-mell** onto the shelf.

Which words mean about the same as **pell-mell**?

- carelessly
- carefully
- sloppily
- neatly
- recklessly

Imagine a room that is organized in a **pell-mell** manner. What does it look like?

negligent

adjective

not showing proper care or concern

Only a **negligent** pet owner would allow a dog to stay outside all day without water.

Which of the following describe **negligent** behavior?

- Tara cleans her fish tank every week.
- While I was talking to my friends, my little brother fell off the slide.
- The dentist told Sandra that she had three cavities and needed to brush and floss her teeth more often.

Give an example of **negligent** behavior that you have seen or heard about. Have you ever been **negligent** about anything?

Week 19
A Word a Day

undeniable

adjective

unquestionably true

After the fierce blizzard, it was **undeniable** that winter had truly arrived.

Which words mean about the same as **undeniable**?

- questionable
- evident
- certain
- obvious
- false

Tell an **undeniable** fact about yourself.

scuffle

noun

a confused struggle or fight

The argument became a **scuffle** when one boy grabbed the other's cap.

Complete this graphic organizer for **scuffle**.

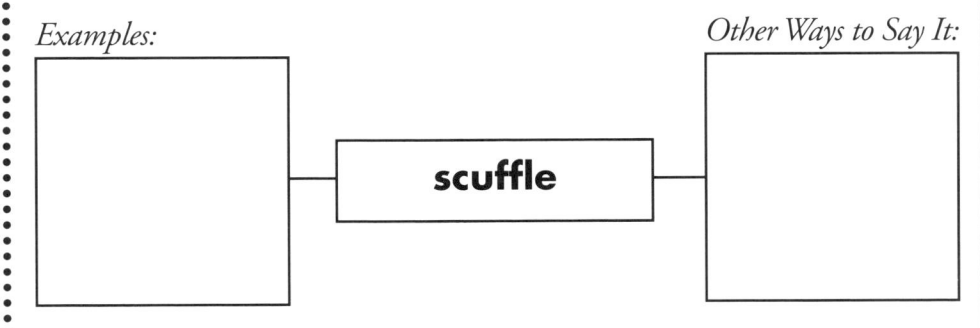

Examples: — **scuffle** — *Other Ways to Say It:*

Where might you see a **scuffle** take place? Have you ever seen a **scuffle**? Where was it?

Review

Week 19
A Word a Day

pell-mell • negligent • undeniable • scuffle

Write on the board the four words studied this week. Read the words with the class and briefly review their meanings. Then conduct the oral activities below.

1 Tell students that you are going to give them a clue about one of the words for the week. They are to find the word that answers the clue.

- This is a fight. **(a scuffle)**
- This word describes people who don't take good care of their pets. **(negligent)**
- This word describes a fact that no one can deny. **(undeniable)**
- Some people don't organize their things. Instead, they just toss them into drawers or closets in this manner. **(pell-mell)**

2 Read each sentence and ask students to supply the correct word to complete the sentence.

- Don't just cram your clothes into your suitcase ____. Fold them neatly. **(pell-mell)**
- The school principal had to break up a ____ today. Luckily, no one was hurt. **(scuffle)**
- Don't be ____. Be sure to put the papers in the recycle bin. **(negligent)**
- After an undefeated season, it was ____ that our team was the best one in the league. **(undeniable)**

3 Read each sentence and ask students to tell which word or words are wrong. Then have them provide the correct word from the week's list.

- Alex tosses unmatched socks into a drawer in an orderly way. **(in an orderly way/pell-mell)**
- We know that the Earth is a sphere. This fact is questionable. **(questionable/undeniable)**
- The careful homeowner did not repair the step, and a visitor fell and broke his ankle. **(careful/negligent)**

4 Read each sentence and ask students to decide if it is true or false. If the sentence is false, instruct students to explain why.

- In a landslide, rocks may roll pell-mell down a hill and onto the road below. **(true)**
- Negligent pet owners should not be allowed to adopt additional pets. **(true)**
- Students are not allowed to have scuffles at school. **(true)**
- *Untrue* and *undeniable* are synonyms. **(false; they are antonyms)**

Answers for page 79: 1. C, 2. J, 3. A, 4. G

Name _____

Week 19
A Word a Day

Review Words   pell-mell • negligent • undeniable • scuffle

Fill in the bubble next to the correct answer.

1. Which sentence describes a *scuffle*?
   - Ⓐ A cat lay curled up on the sofa in the morning sun.
   - Ⓑ A cat stared out the window at several birds in a tree.
   - Ⓒ One cat swatted another, and the two began to wrestle.
   - Ⓓ Side by side, three cats ate hungrily from three bowls.

2. Which word is an antonym for *undeniable*?
   - Ⓕ tolerable
   - Ⓖ provable
   - Ⓗ answerable
   - Ⓙ questionable

3. Which phrase means the opposite of *pell-mell*?
   - Ⓐ in an orderly manner
   - Ⓑ in a hurried way
   - Ⓒ in a sloppy, messy way
   - Ⓓ in a reluctant manner

4. Which is a *negligent* act?
   - Ⓕ giving your dog a bath
   - Ⓖ forgetting to feed your cat
   - Ⓗ taking your dog for a walk
   - Ⓙ taking your cat to the vet

Writing

Write about the messiest room you have ever seen. Use **pell-mell** in your sentences.

_____

_____

_____

© Evan-Moor Corp. • EMC 2795 • A Word a Day

Week 20
A Word a Day

tantalize

verb

to tease with something desirable but withhold it

It is cruel to **tantalize** caged animals with tempting foods.

In which of these situations is someone being **tantalized**?

- Roberto held the toy up out of the reach of his little sister.
- Sarah shared her cookies with her friend Megan.
- That pizza smells so good, but it's not on my diet!
- The cat stared for hours at the bird high in the tree.
- We followed the smell of fried chicken until we found the restaurant.

What can **tantalize** you? What could you use to **tantalize** your best friend?

contemporary

adjective

up-to-date; modern or current

antonym: old

The **contemporary** digital clock looked out of place among the antique furnishings.

Complete this graphic organizer for **contemporary**.

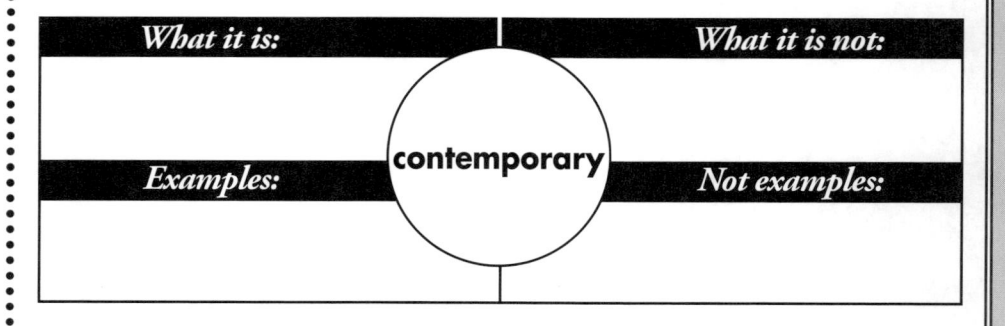

What it is:	What it is not:
Examples:	Not examples:

(center: contemporary)

Describe some items in your home that are **contemporary**.

Week 20
A Word a Day

vicinity

noun

the area nearby

> There are three playgrounds in the **vicinity** of my home.

Which of these things are in the **vicinity** of where you live?

- the Rocky Mountains
- Disney World
- a grocery store
- a park
- a school

Tell the class about some of the unusual things that are in the **vicinity** of your home.

annex

verb

to add or attach to something larger

noun

a wing added to a building

> The hospital had to **annex** a building next door when it opened the new pediatric **annex**.

Which meaning is being described: "to add or attach" or "a wing added to a building"?

- The new annex will give us room for a home office.
- Our school will annex the lot next to it in order to build more classrooms.
- The school added an annex to house a new auditorium.
- The YMCA annexed the warehouse next door and turned it into a gym.
- The United States annexed Texas in 1845.

If you could add an **annex** to your home, what would you use it for?

Review

Week 20
A Word a Day

> tantalize • contemporary • vicinity • annex

Write on the board the four words studied this week. Read the words with the class and briefly review their meanings. Then conduct the oral activities below.

❶ Tell students that you are going to give them a clue about one of the words for the week. They are to find the word that answers the clue.

- This is an addition to a building. **(an annex)**
- This word describes modern art. **(contemporary)**
- Bakery owners do this to their customers by displaying cakes in glass cases. **(tantalize them)**
- Your home and your school are probably in the same one. **(vicinity)**

❷ Read each sentence and ask students to supply the correct word to complete the sentence.

- There is a supermarket in the ____. It's only about a mile from here. **(vicinity)**
- After the hurricane destroyed part of our school, we had to ____ a nearby building until repairs were completed. **(annex)**
- I prefer older home designs to ____ designs. **(contemporary)**
- Please don't ____ me with descriptions of delicious foods when it's a long time until dinner. **(tantalize)**

❸ Read each sentence and ask students to tell which word or words are wrong. Then have them provide the correct word from the week's list.

- Delicious smells disgust restaurant customers. **(disgust/tantalize)**
- The newest phones have the most outdated designs. **(outdated/contemporary)**
- Recently, the hospital added on an original building so that it could serve more patients. **(original building/annex)**

❹ Read each sentence and ask students to decide if it is true or false. If the sentence is false, instruct students to explain why.

- *Annex* and *add* are synonyms. **(true)**
- Los Angeles and New York City are in the same vicinity. **(false; they are several thousand miles apart)**
- *Contemporary* and *modern* are synonyms. **(true)**
- The smell of fish tantalizes cats. **(true)**

Answers for page 83: 1. A, 2. J, 3. C, 4. G

Week 20
A Word a Day

Name _____

Review Words tantalize • contemporary • vicinity • annex

Fill in the bubble next to the correct answer.

1. **Which sentence describes an *annex*?**
   - Ⓐ When the town grew, the school had to add on a new wing.
   - Ⓑ The main school building is two stories high and has 16 classrooms.
   - Ⓒ There is an auditorium, a cafeteria, a gymnasium, and a playground.
   - Ⓓ The principal has hired a new physical education teacher for next year.

2. **Which word or phrase means the opposite of *contemporary*?**
   - Ⓕ deluxe
   - Ⓖ plain
   - Ⓗ fashionable
   - Ⓙ old-fashioned

3. **Something that's in the *vicinity* is ____.**
   - Ⓐ far away
   - Ⓑ 100 miles from here
   - Ⓒ not too far away
   - Ⓓ in the next town

4. **Which word is a synonym for *tantalize*?**
   - Ⓕ please
   - Ⓖ tease
   - Ⓗ critique
   - Ⓙ neglect

Writing

Write about the kind of home you would like to live in when you are an adult. Use **contemporary** in your sentences.

_____
_____
_____

© Evan-Moor Corp. • EMC 2795 • A Word a Day   **83**

Week 21
A Word a Day

brawny

adjective

muscular and strong

synonym: powerful

The **brawny** lumberjack easily sawed through the logs.

Complete this graphic organizer for **brawny**.

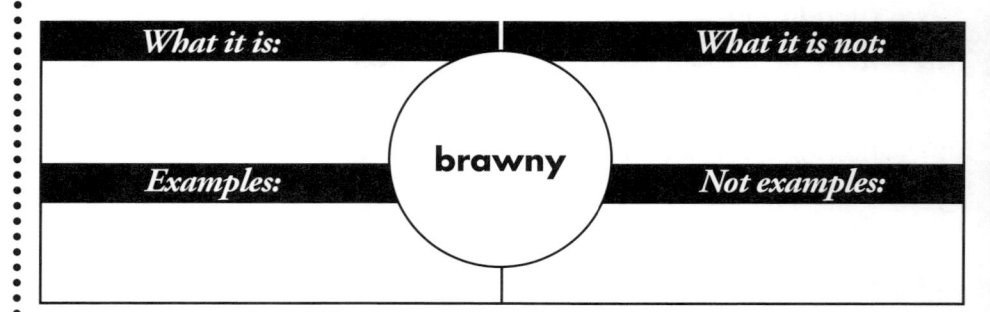

What it is:		What it is not:
	brawny	
Examples:		Not examples:

Describe someone you know who is **brawny**.

curfew

noun

a rule that prevents people from moving around freely after dark

Our community has an eleven o'clock **curfew** for people under sixteen years old.

Which of these would have the authority to set a **curfew** for you?

- the city government
- your mom or dad
- your teacher
- the president
- your friend

Do you think it is a good idea to have a **curfew** for teenagers? Explain your thinking.

Week 21
A Word a Day

radiate

verb

to give off heat or light

> The heat that **radiated** from the campfire almost melted the soles of my sneakers.

Which of the following **radiate**? Do they **radiate** heat or light?

- a fireplace
- a wooden table
- a flashlight that is turned on
- an electric heater
- a glass of water

If someone "**radiates** happiness," what do you think that means? What are some other qualities that people could **radiate**?

prosperous

adjective

having economic well-being

synonym: wealthy

> The **prosperous** business donated thousands of dollars so that a swimming pool could be built at the high school.

Which words mean about the same as **prosperous**?

- impoverished
- successful
- affluent
- broke
- well-off

What are some things that being **prosperous** enables people to do?

Review

Week 21
A Word a Day

brawny • curfew • radiate • prosperous

Write on the board the four words studied this week. Read the words with the class and briefly review their meanings. Then conduct the oral activities below.

❶ Tell students that you are going to give them a clue about one of the words for the week. They are to find the word that answers the clue.

- This is a deadline for coming home at night. **(a curfew)**
- This word could describe a high school football player. **(brawny)**
- Fluorescent lamps do this. **(radiate light)**
- This word describes a successful business. **(prosperous)**

❷ Read each sentence and ask students to supply the correct word to complete the sentence.

- Mr. Boynton's restaurant isn't very ___ these days. In fact, it's losing money. **(prosperous)**
- When Mom was a teenager, her weekend ___ was midnight. **(curfew)**
- A ___ firefighter lifted my grandma as if she weighed no more than a child. **(brawny)**
- Old-fashioned wood-burning stoves can ___ enough heat to substitute for modern furnaces. **(radiate)**

❸ Read each sentence and ask students to tell which word is wrong. Then have them provide the correct word from the week's list.

- Gas lanterns absorb lots of light. **(absorb/radiate)**
- Chloe's unsuccessful business will earn a million dollars by the time she turns thirty. **(unsuccessful/prosperous)**
- You have to be fairly weak to lift 200 pounds. **(weak/brawny)**

❹ Read each sentence and ask students to decide if it is true or false. If the sentence is false, instruct students to explain why.

- A curfew is a mealtime or bedtime. **(false; it's a deadline for coming home at night)**
- Most wrestlers are brawny. **(true)**
- A lit candle radiates both light and heat. **(true)**
- A prosperous family cannot afford to buy luxuries. **(false; the opposite is true)**

Answers for page 87: 1. D, 2. G, 3. B, 4. G

Week 21
A Word a Day

Name _____

Review Words: brawny • curfew • radiate • prosperous

Fill in the bubble next to the correct answer.

1. **Which sentence describes a *curfew*?**
   - Ⓐ On weekend nights, my parents allow me to stay up late.
   - Ⓑ On school days, I have to wake up at 7:00 A.M. to be ready on time.
   - Ⓒ I am usually in bed and asleep by 9:30 P.M. on school nights.
   - Ⓓ My seventeen-year-old sister has to be home by 11:00 P.M. on weekends.

2. **Which word is an antonym for *prosperous*?**
   - Ⓕ unhealthy
   - Ⓖ penniless
   - Ⓗ slender
   - Ⓙ uneducated

3. **Which word is a synonym for *radiate*?**
   - Ⓐ exit
   - Ⓑ glow
   - Ⓒ absorb
   - Ⓓ trickle

4. **Which phrase describes a *brawny* person?**
   - Ⓕ small and frail
   - Ⓖ big and muscular
   - Ⓗ flexible and energetic
   - Ⓙ intelligent and sensible

Writing

Write about people or groups you would help if you were rich. Use **prosperous** in your sentences.

_____

_____

_____

Week 22
A Word a Day

endurance

noun

the ability to withstand stress or hardship

The marathon runner has the **endurance** to run thirty miles.

Complete this graphic organizer for **endurance**.

Examples: — **endurance** — *Other Ways to Say It:*

Describe someone you know who has **endurance**.

inundate

verb

1. to flood or overflow
2. to overrun or overwhelm

The heavy rains caused the river to rise and **inundate** the lowlands. The nearby fields were **inundated** with ants fleeing from the rising water.

Which meaning is being used: "to flood" or "to overwhelm"?

- I am inundated with work.
- Locusts inundated the wheat fields.
- Waves caused by hurricane-force winds inundated the beach community.
- After the cloudburst, our patio was inundated.
- The bride and groom were inundated with wedding gifts.

If your home was about to be **inundated**, what would you grab before leaving?

Week 22
A Word a Day

vital

adjective

necessary for supporting life

antonym: unimportant

Clean air is **vital** to human survival.

Which of the following are **vital** to survival?
- running shoes
- clean water
- computers
- clothing
- food

What are three things that are **vital** in your life?

phenomenon

noun

1. a fact or an event that can be seen or felt
2. something unusual and remarkable

Lightning is a natural **phenomenon** that has always awed people.

The Beatles were a **phenomenon** that thrilled young people during the '60s.

Which meaning is being used: "an observable event" or "something extraordinary"?
- The child was a phenomenon, having mastered six different languages by the age of seven.
- A solar eclipse is a spectacular phenomenon to observe.
- Crowds cheered the returning Olympic phenomenon.
- Tornadoes are a scary phenomenon.
- He is a math phenomenon who can multiply large numbers in his head.

Give an example of someone or something you think is a **phenomenon**.

Review

Week 22
A Word a Day

endurance • inundate • vital • phenomenon

Write on the board the four words studied this week. Read the words with the class and briefly review their meanings. Then conduct the oral activities below.

1 Tell students that you are going to give them a clue about one of the words for the week. They are to find the word that answers the clue.

- Thunder is a natural one. **(phenomenon)**
- Long-distance runners need this. **(endurance)**
- Weeks of heavy rain might do this to a valley. **(inundate it)**
- This word describes needs such as food, clean water, clothing, and shelter. **(vital)**

2 Read each sentence and ask students to supply the correct word to complete the sentence.

- The home computer was a _____ that transformed people's lives, beginning in the 1970s. **(phenomenon)**
- After the hurricane, volunteers transported _____ supplies to the affected area. **(vital)**
- Running a marathon requires extraordinary _____. **(endurance)**
- Mosquitoes _____ our yard on summer evenings, making it impossible to sit outdoors. **(inundate)**

3 Read each sentence and ask students to tell which word is wrong. Then have them provide the correct word from the week's list.

- Water is trivial to human survival. **(trivial/vital)**
- Floodwaters will soon empty the riverbanks. **(empty/inundate)**
- Camels have the weakness required for long-distance treks. **(weakness/endurance)**

4 Read each sentence and ask students to decide if it is true or false. If the sentence is false, instruct students to explain why.

- A phenomenon is imaginary. **(false; a phenomenon is an observable fact or event)**
- A swimming pool is a vital need. **(false; people don't need swimming pools to survive)**
- Olympic swimmers need endurance. **(true)**
- Moviegoers could inundate the only theater where the latest hit movie was playing. **(true)**

Answers for page 91: 1. C, 2. J, 3. C, 4. F

Name _____

Week 22
A Word a Day

Review Words   endurance • inundate • vital • phenomenon

Fill in the bubble next to the correct answer.

1. Which word is an antonym for *vital*?
   - Ⓐ essential
   - Ⓑ fascinating
   - Ⓒ trivial
   - Ⓓ pleasant

2. Which word is a synonym for *endurance*?
   - Ⓕ flimsiness
   - Ⓖ laziness
   - Ⓗ frailty
   - Ⓙ stamina

3. In which sentence is *phenomenon* used correctly?
   - Ⓐ Honesty is the best phenomenon that Katrina possesses.
   - Ⓑ Michael has an irritating phenomenon of interrupting other people.
   - Ⓒ The cellphone is a phenomenon that has changed communication.
   - Ⓓ Jumping six feet into the air is my cat's most impressive phenomenon.

4. Which might *inundate* a city?
   - Ⓕ floodwaters
   - Ⓖ rescue work
   - Ⓗ an election
   - Ⓙ lack of money

Writing

Write about a natural phenomenon that amazes you. Use **phenomenon** in your sentences.

_____

_____

_____

© Evan-Moor Corp. • EMC 2795 • A Word a Day   **91**

Week 23
A Word a Day

jostled

verb

bumped or pushed around roughly

The passengers were **jostled** about when the train came to a sudden stop.

Where might you get **jostled**?

- in a crowded arena
- playing football
- on a roller coaster
- at a bookstore
- playing golf

Describe a situation in which you were **jostled**.

hearty

adjective

full of warmth and friendliness

My grandfather gave us a **hearty** welcome when we arrived.

Which words mean about the same as **hearty**?

- enthusiastic
- cheerful
- tearful
- pitiful
- cold

Whom would you greet with a **hearty** welcome? Who greets you with a **hearty** welcome?

Week 23
A Word a Day

emotion

noun

any strong feeling

> The new father was overcome with **emotion** as he gazed at his infant daughter.

How would you name the **emotions** being described in these situations?

- We jumped around and yelled when our team won.
- Tina sobbed for hours when her puppy was lost.
- Dad grinned from ear to ear when I got my award.
- We huddled in a corner of the basement and waited for the tornado alert to end.
- I could feel my face turning red as the class laughed at my answer.

What is an **emotion** that is difficult for you to control? What is your favorite **emotion**? Explain your answers.

procrastinate

verb

to put off doing something until a future time

> I'd better start writing and not **procrastinate** any longer, because the report is due tomorrow.

Complete this graphic organizer for **procrastinate**.

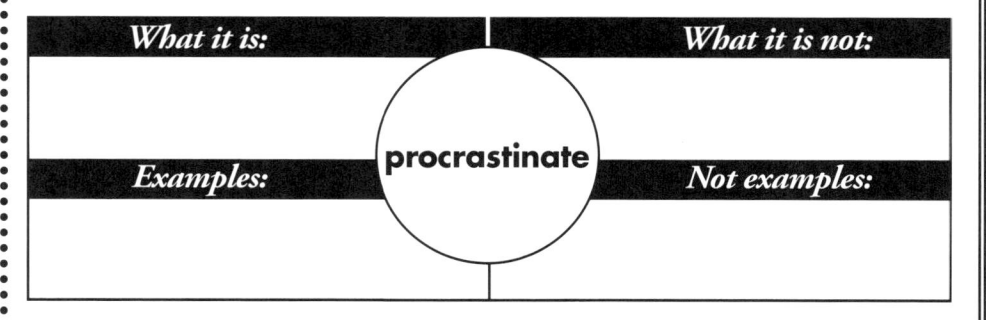

What it is:	What it is not:
Examples:	Not examples:

(center: procrastinate)

Do you think it is a good idea to **procrastinate**? Why or why not?

Review

Week 23
A Word a Day

> jostled • hearty • emotion • procrastinate

Write on the board the four words studied this week. Read the words with the class and briefly review their meanings. Then conduct the oral activities below.

❶ Tell students that you are going to give them a clue about one of the words for the week. They are to find the word that answers the clue.

- This word describes a firm, friendly handshake. (**hearty**)
- Deep sadness is one. Joy is another. (**emotion**)
- If you do this, you may never finish a project. (**procrastinate**)
- Maybe you have accidentally done this to other passengers on a crowded bus. (**jostled them**)

❷ Read each sentence and ask students to supply the correct word to complete the sentence.

- I dropped my backpack when someone ____ me on a crowded subway train. (**jostled**)
- "Great to see you!" called my uncle in a ____ voice. (**hearty**)
- I try not to ____, because I don't like finishing projects at the last moment. (**procrastinate**)
- Everyone was filled with ____ during my cousin's marriage ceremony. (**emotion**)

❸ Read each sentence and ask students to tell which word or words are wrong. Then have them provide the correct word from the week's list.

- "It's wonderful to meet you!" Nick said in a hostile voice. (**hostile/hearty**)
- I always regret it when I complete projects promptly. (**complete projects promptly/procrastinate**)
- "Thank you so much!" Mom said to the firefighters with lack of feeling in her voice. (**lack of feeling/emotion**)

❹ Read each sentence and ask students to decide if it is true or false. If the sentence is false, instruct students to explain why.

- Anger is an emotion. (**true**)
- Procrastinating ensures that you'll complete jobs on time. (**false; the opposite is true**)
- A hearty smile can make you feel welcome. (**true**)
- The last time you jostled someone, you probably didn't do it on purpose. (**true**)

Answers for page 95: 1. D, 2. H, 3. A, 4. G

Name _____

Week 23
A Word a Day

Review Words jostled • hearty • emotion • procrastinate

Fill in the bubble next to the correct answer.

1. **Which word is an antonym for *hearty*?**
   - Ⓐ welcoming
   - Ⓑ slender
   - Ⓒ bizarre
   - Ⓓ feeble

2. **Which group of words name *emotions*?**
   - Ⓕ urge, desire, temptation
   - Ⓖ thought, idea, belief
   - Ⓗ sorrow, joy, fear
   - Ⓙ scheme, plan, intent

3. **In which sentence is *procrastinate* used correctly?**
   - Ⓐ Don't procrastinate, or you will not be able to meet your deadline.
   - Ⓑ Don't procrastinate. It is very important to get enough sleep at night.
   - Ⓒ If you procrastinate, you can complete your project with time to spare.
   - Ⓓ If you procrastinate, you won't have room for a slice of blueberry pie.

4. **In which sentence could *jostled* be used to fill in the blank?**
   - Ⓕ I ____ an aluminum can, completely flattening it.
   - Ⓖ I accidentally ____ Mom, and she spilled her coffee.
   - Ⓗ Water ____ quickly down the drain after I unclogged it.
   - Ⓙ Danny ____ us around San Francisco when we visited him.

Writing

Write about a time when you procrastinated and wished you hadn't done so. Use **procrastinate** in your sentences.

_____
_____
_____

© Evan-Moor Corp. • EMC 2795 • A Word a Day

Week 24
A Word a Day

indication

noun

something that points out or indicates; a sign

The smiling faces were a good **indication** that everyone was having a good time.

Complete this graphic organizer for **indication**.

Examples: — indication — *Other Ways to Say It:*

How can your actions give an **indication** of what your feelings are?

taffeta

noun

a stiff, crisp, shiny fabric made of silk, nylon, or rayon

The ballerina's tutu was made of beautiful lavender **taffeta**.

Which of these might be made from **taffeta**?
- a newborn's nightgown
- a military uniform
- an evening gown
- a wedding gown
- fancy living room drapes

Who might wear a garment made from **taffeta**? On what occasions would the garment be worn?

Week 24
A Word a Day

contribute

verb

to give help or money

The women's organization was able to **contribute** ten thousand dollars for restoring the old schoolhouse.

Which words mean about the same as **contribute**?

- assist
- consider
- donate
- support
- reflect

Have you ever **contributed** time or money to something? What did you do?

humorous

adjective

full of humor; amusing

synonym: funny

People laughed all evening as they enjoyed the **humorous** play.

Which words mean about the same as **humorous**?

- hilarious
- comical
- tragic
- scary
- sad

What is your favorite **humorous** movie?

Review

Week 24
A Word a Day

indication • taffeta • contribute • humorous

Write on the board the four words studied this week. Read the words with the class and briefly review their meanings. Then conduct the oral activities below.

❶ Tell students that you are going to give them a clue about one of the words for the week. They are to find the word that answers the clue.

- This word describes a funny book or movie. **(humorous)**
- You do this when you donate money to charity or work as a volunteer. **(contribute)**
- A bridesmaid's dress might be made from this. **(taffeta)**
- This is a clue or sign that something is true. **(an indication)**

❷ Read each sentence and ask students to supply the correct word to complete the sentence.

- Danny's bad mood was an ____ that something had upset him at school. **(indication)**
- My sister wore a blue ____ gown to her senior prom. **(taffeta)**
- Dad doesn't think it is ____ to play tricks on people. **(humorous)**
- Careful planning will ____ to our school carnival's success. **(contribute)**

❸ Read each list of words and phrases. Ask students to supply the word that fits best with each.

- give, donate, assist, volunteer **(contribute)**
- funny, hilarious, amusing, a barrel of laughs **(humorous)**
- clue, pointer, evidence, sign **(indication)**
- silk, nylon, shiny fabric, fancy cloth **(taffeta)**

❹ Read each sentence and ask students to decide if it is true or false. If the sentence is false, instruct students to explain why.

- A healthy diet and exercise contribute to good health. **(true)**
- Humorous people are usually fun to be around. **(true)**
- Lack of appetite is an indication of illness in animals. **(true)**
- Farmers and grocers store potatoes in large taffeta sacks. **(false; taffeta is a pretty, fancy fabric best suited for dresses and curtains)**

Answers for page 99: 1. B, 2. J, 3. C, 4. G

Name _____

Week 24
A Word a Day

Review Words indication • taffeta • contribute • humorous

Fill in the bubble next to the correct answer.

1. Which word is an antonym for *humorous*?
   - Ⓐ witty
   - Ⓑ serious
   - Ⓒ casual
   - Ⓓ lengthy

2. Which word is a synonym for *contribute*?
   - Ⓕ steal
   - Ⓖ divide
   - Ⓗ purchase
   - Ⓙ donate

3. In which sentence is *indication* used correctly?
   - Ⓐ If you haven't received my indication, I'll send you another one.
   - Ⓑ My favorite indication in this house is its large, sunny bedrooms.
   - Ⓒ Bo's foot-tapping and squirming were indications of his impatience.
   - Ⓓ My dog shows indication by licking my hands and wagging her tail.

4. Who is most likely to be dressed in *taffeta*?
   - Ⓕ a firefighter on duty
   - Ⓖ a girl at a fancy party
   - Ⓗ a doctor in her office
   - Ⓙ a boy playing soccer

Writing

Write about the most humorous sight you can remember seeing. Use **humorous** in your sentences.

_____

_____

_____

© Evan-Moor Corp. • EMC 2795 • A Word a Day

Week 25
A Word a Day

antidote

noun

something that works against the effects of poison

People bitten by poisonous snakes need to be given an **antidote** as soon as possible to prevent serious illness or death.

Which of the following would require an **antidote** if you were to swallow them?

- drain cleaner
- gasoline
- grass clippings
- rose petals
- insect spray

What kinds of **antidotes** do you know about? Have you ever heard of anyone who had to take an **antidote**? If so, what was it for?

loiter

verb

to stand around in a public place doing nothing in particular

The shopping center is locked up at night to prevent **loitering**.

Which word or words mean about the same as **loiter**?

- pass through
- hang around
- move along
- linger
- loaf

What places in our town have rules about **loitering**? Do you think rules against **loitering** are a good idea? Why or why not?

Week 25
A Word a Day

tattered

adjective

broken-down or worn-out

After years of use, the **tattered** leather sofa was finally replaced.

Complete this graphic organizer for **tattered**.

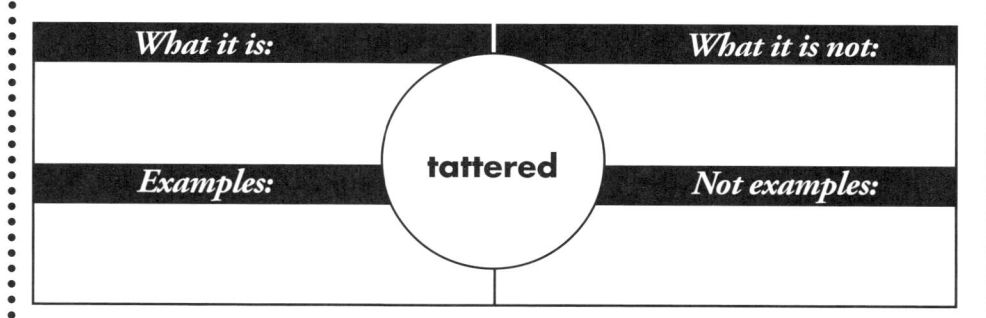

What it is:	What it is not:
Examples:	Not examples:

(center: tattered)

Do you throw out **tattered** things, or do you keep them? Do you repair them, or leave them **tattered**? Describe something you have that is **tattered**.

exquisite

adjective

of exceptional beauty; finely made

The **exquisite** embroidery must have taken hours to complete.

Which words mean about the same as **exquisite**?

- valueless
- elegant
- precious
- crude
- stunning

What is something **exquisite** that you have seen? Describe it.

Review

Week 25
A Word a Day

antidote • loiter • tattered • exquisite

Write on the board the four words studied this week. Read the words with the class and briefly review their meanings. Then conduct the oral activities below.

❶ Tell students that you are going to give them a clue about one of the words for the week. They are to find the word that answers the clue.

- You could use this word to describe a jewel-studded crown. **(exquisite)**
- People do this when they stand around doing nothing. **(loiter)**
- You could use this word to describe an old, worn-out pair of jeans. **(tattered)**
- This could save someone's life. **(an antidote)**

❷ Read each sentence and ask students to supply the correct word to complete the sentence.

- Since we have four cats that love to scratch furniture, it is no wonder that our sofa is ___. **(tattered)**
- This antique dresser has ___ carving on it. **(exquisite)**
- What is an effective ___ for a rattlesnake's bite? **(antidote)**
- Some business owners don't like groups of teens to ___ outside their stores. **(loiter)**

❸ Read each sentence and ask students to tell which word is wrong. Then have them provide the correct word from the week's list.

- Rob likes to wear brand-new shirts that are faded and stained. **(brand-new/tattered)**
- I love the hideous patterns on this mosaic table. **(hideous/exquisite)**
- Quick! Take this poison—it may save your life! **(poison/antidote)**

❹ Read each sentence and ask students to decide if it is true or false. If the sentence is false, instruct students to explain why.

- Most people think that diamonds are exquisite. **(true)**
- People take antidotes to relieve headache pain. **(false; antidotes work against poisons such as snake venom)**
- Cloth-covered furniture can grow tattered if it is left outside for a long time. **(true)**
- Some communities have laws against loitering. **(true)**

Answers for page 103: 1. D, 2. H, 3. B, 4. F

Name _____

Week 25
A Word a Day

Review Words   antidote • loiter • tattered • exquisite

Fill in the bubble next to the correct answer.

1. Where might a person *loiter*?
   - Ⓐ at a friend's house
   - Ⓑ in a classroom
   - Ⓒ in the living room
   - Ⓓ at a mall

2. Which word is a synonym for *exquisite*?
   - Ⓕ pale
   - Ⓖ smooth
   - Ⓗ beautiful
   - Ⓙ soft

3. When is it necessary to take an *antidote*?
   - Ⓐ when you have a terrible headache
   - Ⓑ when a poisonous snake has bitten you
   - Ⓒ when you have a cold, a cough, or the flu
   - Ⓓ when you have a sprain or a broken bone

4. Which of the following is most likely to be *tattered*?
   - Ⓕ your favorite baby blanket
   - Ⓖ a sweater you bought a month ago
   - Ⓗ a bike you received for your last birthday
   - Ⓙ this morning's newspaper

Writing

Write about the oldest piece of clothing that you own. Use **tattered** in your sentences.

_____

_____

_____

© Evan-Moor Corp. • EMC 2795 • A Word a Day

Week 26
A Word a Day

Spartan

adjective

strictly self-disciplined; not easy or comfortable

> The wrestler followed a **Spartan** routine in his training, working out three hours every day.

Which words mean about the same as **Spartan**?

- self-restrained
- delicate
- severe
- stern
- weak

The word **Spartan** is derived from ancient Sparta, where warriors were known for bravery and self-discipline. Could you follow a **Spartan** training routine? Do you think having self-discipline is a good idea? Why or why not?

recoil

verb

to draw back in fear or disgust

> We saw the dog **recoil** as it came across a rattlesnake on the path.

Complete this graphic organizer for **recoil**.

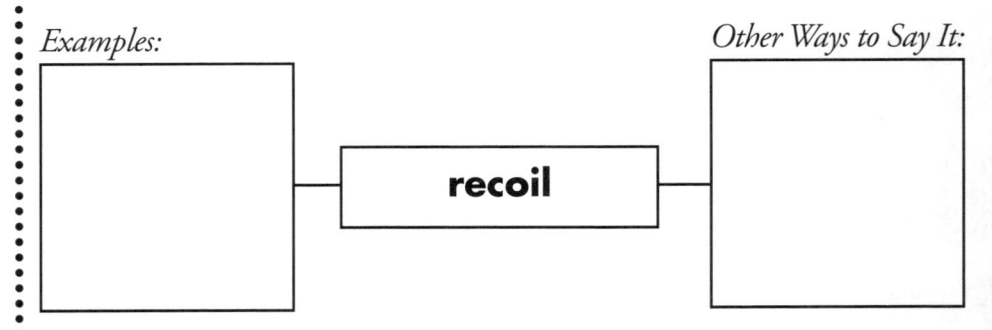

Examples: □ — **recoil** — □ *Other Ways to Say It:*

What is something that would make you **recoil**? Why?

Week 26
A Word a Day

abominable

adjective

something hideous and unappealing

synonym: disgusting

As we approached the garbage dump, the **abominable** odor nearly knocked me out!

Which words mean about the same as **abominable**?

- atrocious
- pleasant
- offensive
- lovely
- nasty

Give an example of something you consider to be **abominable**.

native

noun

a person born or raised in a particular place

My grandmother is a **native** of the Philippines, and she returns there every year.

Which words mean about the same as **native**?

- foreigner
- resident
- citizen
- local
- immigrant

Is there anyone in your family who is a **native** of another country? Which country?

Review

Week 26
A Word a Day

Spartan • recoil • abominable • native

Write on the board the four words studied this week. Read the words with the class and briefly review their meanings. Then conduct the oral activities below.

❶ Tell students that you are going to give them a clue about one of the words for the week. They are to find the word that answers the clue.

- You could use this word to describe criminal behavior. **(abominable)**
- You might do this if you suddenly saw something scary right in front of you. **(recoil)**
- You could use this word to describe a serious student's studying schedule. **(Spartan)**
- If you were born in the United States, you are a U.S. one of these. **(native)**

❷ Read each sentence and ask students to supply the correct word to complete the sentence.

- Since I was born in Los Angeles, I am a California ___. **(native)**
- Even our coach recommends an occasional break from our ___ training routine. **(Spartan)**
- Seeing a huge spider in the bathtub made me ___ when I pulled back the shower curtain. **(recoil)**
- My parents won't let me watch movies that have ___ violence in them. **(abominable)**

❸ Read each sentence and ask students to tell which word or words are wrong. Then have them provide the correct word from the week's list.

- Mark's lazy routine includes waking up at six o'clock each day, even on weekends. **(lazy/Spartan)**
- Molly is a foreigner who was born right here in our town. **(foreigner/native)**
- You really must do something about your admirable table manners! **(admirable/abominable)**
- I couldn't help but march on when I saw the huge crocodile on the bank of the river. **(march on/recoil)**

❹ Read each sentence and ask students to decide if it is true or false. If the sentence is false, instruct students to explain why.

- A U.S. native may have parents from another nation. **(true)**
- It takes self-discipline to live a Spartan lifestyle. **(true)**
- Recoiling is the same as springing forward. **(false; to recoil means to move back—in fear or disgust, for example)**
- Rotten eggs have an abominable odor. **(true)**

Answers for page 107: 1. C, 2. J, 3. A, 4. G

106

Week 26
A Word a Day

Name _____

Review Words Spartan • recoil • abominable • native

Fill in the bubble next to the correct answer.

1. Which phrase is an antonym for *recoil*?
   - Ⓐ stretch out
   - Ⓑ squat down
   - Ⓒ lunge forward
   - Ⓓ shrink back

2. Which word is a synonym for *abominable*?
   - Ⓕ bleached
   - Ⓖ plump
   - Ⓗ frozen
   - Ⓙ hideous

3. Which person is a United States *native*?
   - Ⓐ Julie, who has Canadian parents and was born in California
   - Ⓑ Ross, who has English parents and was born in Canada
   - Ⓒ Paul, who was born in the Philippines and is now a U.S. citizen
   - Ⓓ Lily, who was born in Cambodia and is now a U.S. resident

4. In which sentence could *Spartan* be used to fill in the blank?
   - Ⓕ Hollie is a ____ dog that spends most of her time eating or napping.
   - Ⓖ Our ____ training schedule begins with a four-mile run before breakfast.
   - Ⓗ My ____ parents allow me to decide when it is time to clean my bedroom.
   - Ⓙ Last night, I saw a ____ film that was the funniest movie I've ever seen.

Writing

Write about the most abominable odor that you have ever smelled. Use **abominable** in your sentences.

_____

_____

_____

Week 27
A Word a Day

disheveled

adjective

untidy; rumpled

After my brother and I finished a bedtime pillow fight, both of our beds were **disheveled**.

Which words mean about the same as **disheveled**?

- in disarray
- disorderly
- organized
- untidy
- clean

Name some things that can appear **disheveled**.

pandemonium

noun

a wild uproar

There was **pandemonium** in the stadium when the home team won the championship game.

Complete this graphic organizer for **pandemonium**.

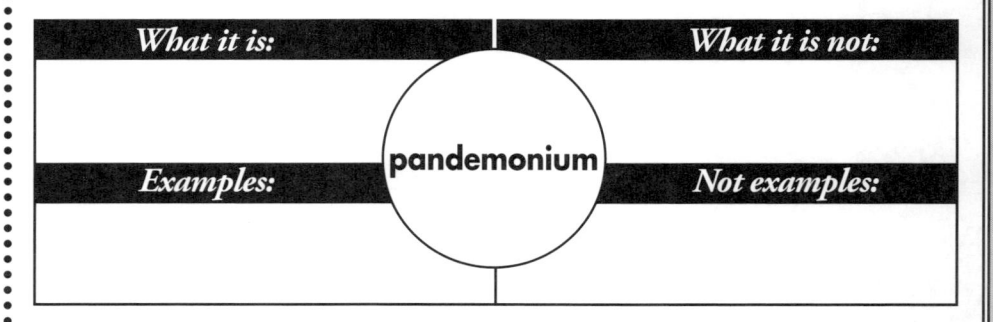

What it is:		What it is not:
Examples:	pandemonium	Not examples:

Where might you see **pandemonium** occur?

Week 27
A Word a Day

terminate

verb

to bring to an end

We had to **terminate** our bike ride when it began to rain heavily.

Which words mean about the same as **terminate**?
- conclude
- complete
- begin
- finish
- start

If you could choose to **terminate** something, what would it be?

pungent

adjective

sharp or strong to the senses of taste or smell

The **pungent** odor of fish could be smelled from one end of the wharf to the other.

Which of these foods might have **pungent** smells or tastes?
- a chocolate chip cookie
- certain cheeses
- sauerkraut
- mashed potatoes
- fish stew

Name some other things that can be **pungent**.

Review

Week 27
A Word a Day

disheveled • pandemonium • terminate • pungent

Write on the board the four words studied this week. Read the words with the class and briefly review their meanings. Then conduct the oral activities below.

❶ Tell students that you are going to give them a clue about one of the words for the week. They are to find the word that answers the clue.

- You could use this word to describe strong-smelling mustard. **(pungent)**
- It is hard to hold a conversation if this occurs. **(pandemonium)**
- If a worker does her job badly, her boss might do this to her employment. **(terminate it)**
- Your hair looks this way when you wake up. **(disheveled)**

❷ Read each sentence and ask students to supply the correct word to complete the sentence.

- A ___ smell of frying onions came from the restaurant kitchen. **(pungent)**
- As soon as the rock group stopped playing, ___ broke out in the audience. **(pandemonium)**
- Sleeping on a plane makes my clothes look ___. **(disheveled)**
- A fire drill made it necessary to ___ the lesson. **(terminate)**

❸ Read each sentence and ask students to tell which word or words are wrong. Then have them provide the correct word from the week's list.

- There was silence on the playground as the students left for summer vacation. **(silence/pandemonium)**
- I must begin our conversation, as I need to leave to catch the bus. **(begin/terminate)**
- When I pulled a shirt out of the pile of dirty clothes, it looked neat and clean. **(neat and clean/disheveled)**
- Garlic has a mild smell. **(mild/pungent)**

❹ Read each sentence and ask students to decide if it is true or false. If the sentence is false, instruct students to explain why.

- Your bedding looks disheveled until you make your bed. **(true)**
- *Pandemonium* and *uproar* are synonyms. **(true)**
- Most curry tastes pungent. **(true)**
- *Terminate* and *end* are antonyms. **(false; they are synonyms)**

Answers for page 111: 1. A, 2. H, 3. B, 4. J

Week 27
A Word a Day

Name _____

Review Words: disheveled • pandemonium • terminate • pungent

Fill in the bubble next to the correct answer.

1. Which word is an antonym for *pungent*?
   - Ⓐ mild
   - Ⓑ sour
   - Ⓒ rich
   - Ⓓ unappetizing

2. Which word is a synonym for *disheveled*?
   - Ⓕ curly
   - Ⓖ shiny
   - Ⓗ rumpled
   - Ⓙ tidy

3. In which sentence is *terminate* used correctly?
   - Ⓐ Can we terminate today's meeting until next Monday?
   - Ⓑ The conference will begin on Monday and terminate on Thursday.
   - Ⓒ Adding another song will terminate the show from 40 to 60 minutes.
   - Ⓓ I cannot terminate even one more minute of this terrible TV show.

4. Where or when would you be least likely to experience *pandemonium*?
   - Ⓕ at a crowded swimming pool
   - Ⓖ when people are trying to get a movie star's autograph
   - Ⓗ when a team wins the soccer championship
   - Ⓙ at a formal wedding ceremony

Writing

Write about a time when you looked disheveled. Use **disheveled** in your sentences.

_____

_____

_____

Week 28
A Word a Day

pedigree

noun

a list of ancestors of a person or an animal

Our puppy was expensive because his **pedigree** includes several champion show dogs.

Which words mean about the same as **pedigree**?

- ancestry
- offspring
- bloodline
- degree
- lineage

Do you think it's better to have a pet with a **pedigree**? Explain your answer.

condemn

verb

to express strong disapproval

Our school **condemns** all bullying.

Which words mean about the same as **condemn**?

- praise
- deplore
- denounce
- applaud
- censure

Give an example of something you would **condemn**.
Give some examples of actions your school **condemns**.

Week 28
A Word a Day

chronic

adjective

1. lasting a long time; occurring repeatedly
2. done by habit

> My grandma has **chronic** arthritis pain. Instead of being a **chronic** complainer, she uses pain medication.

Which of the following are **chronic** conditions?

- a cold
- asthma
- allergies
- sneezing
- poison oak

Do you have a **chronic** worry about anything? Does anyone you know have a **chronic** worry? What causes the worry?

leisure

noun

freedom from work or other duties; free time

> When I get home from work, I spend much of my **leisure** time playing with my dogs.

Complete this graphic organizer for **leisure**.

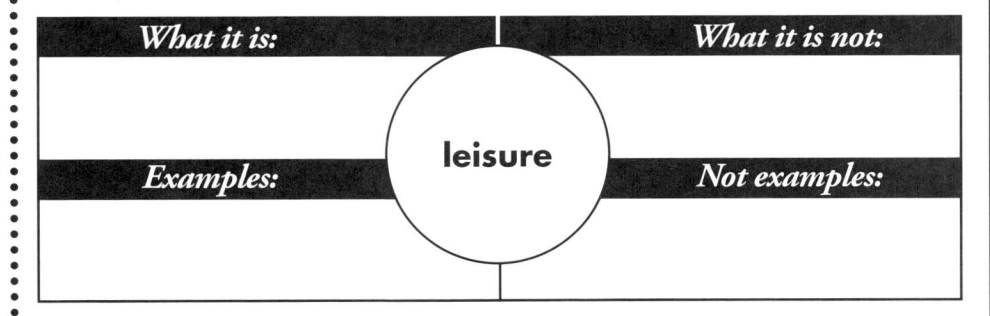

What it is:	What it is not:
Examples:	Not examples:

(center: leisure)

What do you like to do for **leisure**?

Review

Week 28
A Word a Day

pedigree • condemn • chronic • leisure

Write on the board the four words studied this week. Read the words with the class and briefly review their meanings. Then conduct the oral activities below.

1 Tell students that you are going to give them a clue about one of the words for the week. They are to find the word that answers the clue.

- Most people have some during weekends. **(leisure time)**
- A show dog has one. **(a pedigree)**
- This word describes an ongoing medical condition. **(chronic)**
- You would probably do this if a friend stole something or lied to you. **(condemn the behavior)**

2 Read each sentence and ask students to supply the correct word to complete the sentence.

- I ___ behavior such as lying, cheating, and stealing. **(condemn)**
- I'm looking forward to having plenty of ___ during the summertime. **(leisure)**
- Cheryl's baby sister is a ___ thumb-sucker. **(chronic)**
- We adopted our mixed-breed dog from an animal shelter. Obviously, she has no known ___. **(pedigree)**

3 Read each sentence and ask students to tell which word or words are wrong. Then have them provide the correct word from the week's list.

- Danny has a temporary sinus condition that has bothered him for years. **(temporary/chronic)**
- I can relax and daydream when I am at work. **(work/leisure)**
- Most cultures strongly approve of murder. **(approve of/condemn)**

4 Read each sentence and ask students to decide if it is true or false. If the sentence is false, instruct students to explain why.

- Most purebred dogs have pedigrees. **(true)**
- Ignoring bad behavior is the same as condemning it. **(false; when you condemn bad behavior, you say or show that you believe it is wrong)**
- Most people need leisure. **(true)**
- *Chronic* and *habitual* are antonyms. **(false; they are synonyms)**

Answers for page 115: 1. D, 2. G, 3. D, 4. H

Week 28
A Word a Day

Name _____

Review Words   pedigree • condemn • chronic • leisure

Fill in the bubble next to the correct answer.

1. Which word is an antonym for *condemn*?
   Ⓐ dislike
   Ⓑ forbid
   Ⓒ fear
   Ⓓ admire

2. Which word is a synonym for *pedigree*?
   Ⓕ childhood
   Ⓖ ancestry
   Ⓗ appearance
   Ⓙ personality

3. Which activity might someone do when he or she has *leisure*?
   Ⓐ take out the trash
   Ⓑ complete a school project
   Ⓒ vacuum the living room rug
   Ⓓ have a picnic at the beach

4. In which sentence is *chronic* used correctly?
   Ⓕ Fleabites and mosquito bites cause chronic, itchy swelling.
   Ⓖ Grandpa's wound was so chronic that he needed surgery.
   Ⓗ Ever since I was little, my mom has had chronic back pain.
   Ⓙ Last week I had a chronic case of the flu, but I'm better now.

Writing

Write about a habit of yours that you would like to break. Use **chronic** in your sentences.

_____
_____
_____

Week 29
A Word a Day

retaliate

verb

to strike back;
to get revenge

It's best to avoid a bully. You could get hurt if you try to **retaliate**.

Complete this graphic organizer for **retaliate**.

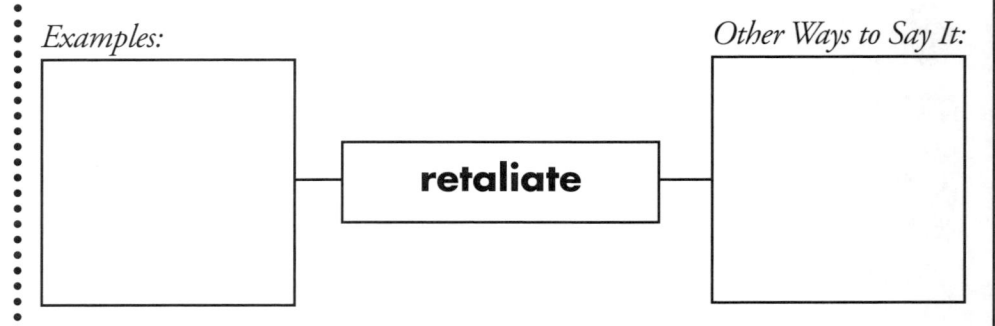

Examples: — **retaliate** — *Other Ways to Say It:*

Do you think it's ever a good idea to **retaliate**? Explain your thinking.

translucent

adjective

allowing only some light to pass through so that images can't be seen clearly

Most bathroom windows are **translucent** to ensure privacy, but let some light in.

Which of these materials could be **translucent**?

- plastic
- wood
- paper
- glass
- iron

Point out something **translucent** in our classroom or somewhere else at school.

Week 29
A Word a Day

jut

verb

to stick out sharply

The ocean scenery along this part of the coast is made more interesting by rocks that **jut** out of the water.

Which of the following can be described using the word **jut**?

- the cabinet sticking out from the wall
- a pillow lying in the corner of the couch
- a piece of land that pokes out into a lake
- a skyscraper that rises above other buildings
- a baby bird peeking out of its nest

Describe a geographical feature in our area that **juts** into space or the water.

asset

noun

something valuable or useful

Her great speed combined with endurance was a wonderful **asset** to the track team.

Which of these could be **assets**?

- strength
- selfishness
- a bad temper
- lots of money
- a good memory

What is an **asset** that you or someone else brings to our classroom or community?

Review

Week 29
A Word a Day

retaliate • translucent • jut • asset

Write on the board the four words studied this week. Read the words with the class and briefly review their meanings. Then conduct the oral activities below.

❶ Tell students that you are going to give them a clue about one of the words for the week. They are to find the word that answers the clue.

- A rhinoceros's horn does this in relation to its nose. **(juts out)**
- This word describes frosted glass. **(translucent)**
- Intelligence is one. Money in the bank is another. **(an asset)**
- You may want to do this if someone plays a practical joke on you. **(retaliate)**

❷ Read each sentence and ask students to supply the correct word to complete the sentence.

- An ability to make friends easily is a great _____ to a salesperson. **(asset)**
- Peninsulas, such as Florida, are landmasses that _____ out into the ocean. **(jut)**
- This _____ glass lets in light, but it also provides privacy. **(translucent)**
- Whenever my brother plays a trick on me, I _____ by playing a trick on him. **(retaliate)**

❸ Read each sentence and ask students to tell which word or words are wrong. Then have them provide the correct word from the week's list.

- This company's staff of well-educated employees is a definite problem. **(problem/asset)**
- Golden light shines through the opaque stained-glass window. **(opaque/translucent)**
- During World War II, the Germans bombed England, so the English bombed Germany to make peace. **(make peace/retaliate)**

❹ Read each sentence and ask students to decide if it is true or false. If the sentence is false, instruct students to explain why.

- A cave juts out from a mountainside. **(false; a cave doesn't stick out—it is an opening or a cavern)**
- An asset is a plus. **(true)**
- Enemies are likely to retaliate against each other. **(true)**
- Clear glass is translucent. **(false; it is transparent)**

Answers for page 119: 1. D, 2. F, 3. B, 4. H

Week 29
A Word a Day

Name _____

Review Words: retaliate • translucent • jut • asset

Fill in the bubble next to the correct answer.

1. Which of these is most likely to be *translucent*?
   - Ⓐ lenses for eyeglasses
   - Ⓑ a blindfold
   - Ⓒ a sleeping mask
   - Ⓓ a lampshade

2. Which of these does not *jut* out?
   - Ⓕ a page in a book
   - Ⓖ a swordfish's bill
   - Ⓗ a man's large nose
   - Ⓙ a second-floor balcony

3. Which of these would not be an *asset* to a store?
   - Ⓐ good customers
   - Ⓑ rude workers
   - Ⓒ high profits
   - Ⓓ a great location

4. Which word is an antonym for *retaliate*?
   - Ⓕ destroy
   - Ⓖ avenge
   - Ⓗ forgive
   - Ⓙ reject

Writing

Write about your most useful asset. Use **asset** in your sentences.

_____

_____

Week 30
A Word a Day

immerse

verb

1. to involve or occupy completely
2. to cover completely with water or liquid

She was so **immersed** in the magazine she was reading that she **immersed** her sleeve in her bowl of soup.

Which meaning is being used: "covered with water" or "completely involved"?

- To pass the test, the student immersed himself in study.
- I was so immersed in the movie that I did not hear the phone ring.
- I stepped in a puddle, immersing my shoes in cold water.
- Immerse the sponge in soapy water to wash the counter.
- Hector immerses himself in each new hobby; last year it was skateboarding, and this year it's playing guitar.

What is something that you like to **immerse** yourself in?

temptation

noun

something that tempts or attracts

It was so hot that I could not fight the **temptation** to jump into the cool water.

Which of these might be **temptations** for you?

- a spoonful of medicine
- a cold glass of soda
- a chocolate sundae
- a piece of pizza
- liver and onions

What is a **temptation** that you can't resist?

Week 30
A Word a Day

ravenous

adjective

very hungry

The **ravenous** kittens all fought for a place at the saucer of milk.

Which words mean about the same as **ravenous**?

- full
- raving
- starved
- famished
- disinterested

What do you like to eat when you are feeling **ravenous**?

facilitate

verb

to make less difficult; to help to progress

The outdoor drop box **facilitates** the return of library materials.

Complete this graphic organizer for **facilitate**.

Examples: — **facilitate** — *Other Ways to Say It:*

What is something that **facilitates** doing your homework at home? What **facilitates** doing your work in school?

Review

Week 30
A Word a Day

immerse • temptation • ravenous • facilitate

Write on the board the four words studied this week. Read the words with the class and briefly review their meanings. Then conduct the oral activities below.

1 Tell students that you are going to give them a clue about one of the words for the week. They are to find the word that answers the clue.

- You would probably feel this way if you didn't eat for a whole day. (**ravenous**)
- This is what you do when you put something in water. (**immerse it**)
- This is something that is very hard to resist. (**a temptation**)
- If you need to find information, an Internet search engine can do this for you. (**facilitate the search process**)

2 Read each sentence and ask students to supply the correct word to complete the sentence.

- Since I hadn't had lunch, I felt ___ by dinnertime. (**ravenous**)
- Dad asked me to wait until after dinner, but the ___ to eat some freshly baked cookies before dinner was too great. (**temptation**)
- When I ___ myself in a story, I can't stop reading until I've finished the book. (**immerse**)
- Librarians ___ the process of borrowing books. (**facilitate**)

3 Read each sentence and ask students to tell which word or words are wrong. Then have them provide the correct word from the week's list.

- The Internet prevents information searches. (**prevents/facilitates**)
- Delicious cooking smells make me feel full. (**full/ravenous**)
- These dirty dishes need to soak. Please remove them from the soapy water. (**remove them from/immerse them in**)

4 Read each sentence and ask students to decide if it is true or false. If the sentence is false, instruct students to explain why.

- Something that tantalizes you is a temptation. (**true**)
- Most people feel ravenous after a big meal. (**false; the opposite is true—they feel full**)
- *Immersed* and *involved* are synonyms. (**true**)
- *Facilitate* and *enable* are synonyms. (**true**)

Answers for page 123: 1. C, 2. H, 3. C, 4. F

Name _____

Week 30
A Word a Day

Review Words: immerse • temptation • ravenous • facilitate

Fill in the bubble next to the correct answer.

1. Which word is an antonym for *facilitate*?
   - Ⓐ examine
   - Ⓑ instruct
   - Ⓒ block
   - Ⓓ enable

2. Which of these should you never *immerse* in water?
   - Ⓕ a drinking glass
   - Ⓖ a waterproof watch
   - Ⓗ an electric toaster
   - Ⓙ a set of bedsheets

3. Which of these would not be a *temptation* for most people?
   - Ⓐ buying an ice-cream cone on a hot day
   - Ⓑ spending a little too much money on shoes
   - Ⓒ going swimming on a snowy winter day
   - Ⓓ eating too much Thanksgiving dinner

4. Which word is a synonym for *ravenous*?
   - Ⓕ starving
   - Ⓖ furious
   - Ⓗ fierce
   - Ⓙ rapid

Writing

Write about a time when you became completely involved in an activity or a hobby. Use **immerse** or **immersed** in your sentences.

_____
_____
_____

Week 31
A Word a Day

condense

verb

1. to change from a gas to a liquid
2. to make shorter or more concise

My report on how water vapor in the air **condenses** to make rain is too lengthy. My teacher said I must **condense** it to two pages.

Which meaning is being described: "to change from gas to liquid" or "to make shorter"?

- Please limit your speech to ten minutes.
- I have only a minute left on my phone card, so I can make only a short call.
- There is dew on the grass this morning.
- The steamy shower made the windows fog up.
- The newscast is shorter tonight because the president is giving a televised speech.

Name some words that mean about the same as **condense**, or to make smaller.

dormant

adjective

not active; sleeping

The volcano has been **dormant** for hundreds of years.

Complete this graphic organizer for **dormant**.

Examples: — **dormant** — *Other Ways to Say It:*

Name some plants or animals that can be **dormant**. What other things in nature can be **dormant**?

Week 31
A Word a Day

remote

adjective

1. far away
2. small; slight

> The cabin was in a **remote** location about 25 miles from the nearest town. There was a **remote** chance that visitors would drop by.

Which meaning is being described: "far away" or "slight"?

- The cellphone won't work when we are camping in the mountains.
- To finish writing her novel, the writer moved to a cabin in the mountains.
- There's not much chance they will cancel the game unless there is a sudden storm.
- If I don't learn to accurately catch every ball, I have little chance of making the team.
- The explorer had little chance of surviving once his food ran out.

Name places you know of that are in **remote** locations.

extravagant

adjective

spending lots of money in a free and careless way

> He was **extravagant** in his purchase of expensive gifts for his friends.

Which words mean about the same as **extravagant**?

- excessive
- wasteful
- lavish
- stingy
- thrifty

What is something **extravagant** that you would buy if you had extra money?

Review

Week 31
A Word a Day

condense • dormant • remote • extravagant

Write on the board the four words studied this week. Read the words with the class and briefly review their meanings. Then conduct the oral activities below.

❶ Tell students that you are going to give them a clue about one of the words for the week. They are to find the word that answers the clue.

- This word might describe a hibernating animal. **(dormant)**
- Water vapor in clouds does this to make rain. **(condenses)**
- This word describes a slight chance. **(remote)**
- This word describes someone who isn't thrifty. **(extravagant)**

❷ Read each sentence and ask students to supply the correct word to complete the sentence.

- The hermit lived in a ___ spot many miles from town. **(remote)**
- Some fish species lie ___ during the winter. **(dormant)**
- Do you think it is ___ to pay this much for a pair of jeans? **(extravagant)**
- Whenever someone takes a hot shower, steam ___ on the bathroom mirror. **(condenses)**

❸ Read each sentence and ask students to tell which word or words are wrong. Then have them provide the correct word from the week's list.

- I think it's much too thrifty to buy three pairs of shoes at a time. **(thrifty/extravagant)**
- Villagers built homes on the slopes of the active volcano. **(active/dormant)**
- We need to find a new home. This one is too close to friends, family, school, and workplaces. **(close to/remote from)**
- Sometimes writers lengthen their books so that people can read them in less time. **(lengthen/condense)**

❹ Read each sentence and ask students to decide if it is true or false. If the sentence is false, instruct students to explain why.

- A condensed report has been shortened. **(true)**
- If you are one of thousands who enter a contest, there is a remote chance that you will win. **(true)**
- *Dormant* and *active* are synonyms. **(false; they are antonyms)**
- Extravagant people are misers. **(false; they are spendthrifts)**

Answers for page 127: 1. A, 2. G, 3. A, 4. J

Name _____

Week 31
A Word a Day

Review Words condense • dormant • remote • extravagant

Fill in the bubble next to the correct answer.

1. Which word is an antonym for *extravagant*?
   - Ⓐ thrifty
   - Ⓑ silent
   - Ⓒ risky
   - Ⓓ pale

2. Which of these probably leads to something *condensing*?
   - Ⓕ writing an e-mail to a friend
   - Ⓖ leaving a glass of ice water on the counter
   - Ⓗ arriving late to school
   - Ⓙ locking the front door

3. Which word is an antonym for *dormant*?
   - Ⓐ active
   - Ⓑ asleep
   - Ⓒ closed
   - Ⓓ hungry

4. In which sentence is *remote* used correctly?
   - Ⓕ We live on a remote street that is close to my school and Mom's work.
   - Ⓖ Last summer, we stayed in a remote hotel in downtown San Francisco.
   - Ⓗ We can't buy this remote building—it would be too expensive to repair.
   - Ⓙ We live in a remote location that is fifty miles from the nearest hospital.

Writing

Write about a time when you made an extravagant purchase. Tell whether you regretted it later. Use **extravagant** in your sentences.

_____

_____

Week 32
A Word a Day

tousled

adjective

in a tangled mass

Her hair was **tousled** after riding in the convertible.

Which words mean about the same as **tousled**?

- snarled
- tidy
- messy
- disheveled
- immaculate

When is your hair **tousled**? What do you do to make it look neat again?

perceive

verb

to become aware of something by experiencing it through the senses

We could barely **perceive** the bird's song over the roar of the waterfall.

Which of the following could you **perceive**?

- people speaking a mile away
- images on a movie screen
- roots growing underground
- the smell of burnt toast
- a baby crying in her crib

Is it easier for you to **perceive** things that you see or things that you hear?

Week 32
A Word a Day

overwhelmed

verb
overpowered or made helpless

adjective
burdened or loaded with an excess of something

Huge waves **overwhelmed** the boat. The sailors were **overwhelmed** with relief when the Coast Guard came to rescue them.

Which meaning is being used: "to overpower" or "to burden"?
- Rufus was overwhelmed by the amount of homework he had to finish for the next day.
- Our basketball team overwhelmed the competition by 50 points.
- The idea of moving 2,000 miles away overwhelmed Joe.
- The immense grizzly bear can easily overwhelm its prey.
- The outpouring of help from the community overwhelmed the victims of the tragic fire.

Have you ever felt **overwhelmed**? What was happening? What did you do to feel like you were back in control?

fluctuate

verb
to shift back and forth uncertainly

The weather seemed to **fluctuate** daily, which made it hard to schedule the beach party.

Complete this graphic organizer for **fluctuate**.

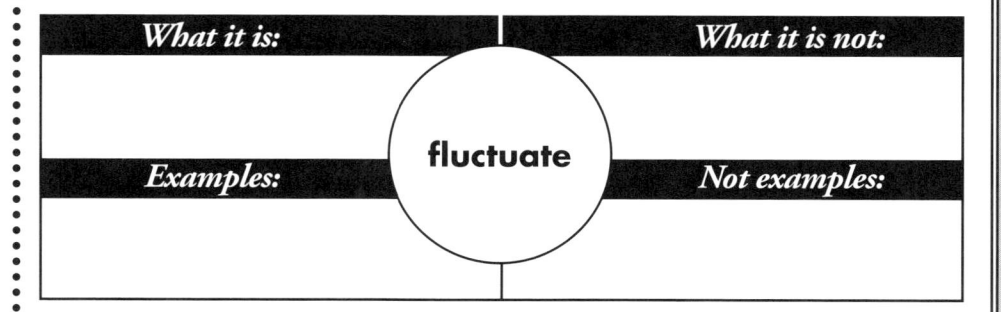

What it is:	What it is not:
Examples:	Not examples:

(center: fluctuate)

Besides the weather, what can **fluctuate**?

Review

Week 32
A Word a Day

tousled • perceive • overwhelmed • fluctuate

Write on the board the four words studied this week. Read the words with the class and briefly review their meanings. Then conduct the oral activities below.

❶ Tell students that you are going to give them a clue about one of the words for the week. They are to find the word that answers the clue.

- Your five senses allow you to do this. **(perceive things)**
- Temperatures often do this in springtime. **(fluctuate)**
- This word describes tangled hair. **(tousled)**
- By the end of the American Civil War, the Union army had done this to the Confederate army. **(overwhelmed it)**

❷ Read each sentence and ask students to supply the correct word to complete the sentence.

- Tonya's problems ___ her, and she began to cry. **(overwhelmed)**
- This morning, I woke up with ___ hair. **(tousled)**
- I ___ that this color is pale green, not yellow. **(perceive)**
- When you have the flu, your temperature may ___ between extremely high and normal. **(fluctuate)**

❸ Read each sentence and ask students to tell which word or words are wrong. Then have them provide the correct word from the week's list.

- Before her mom combed it, little Eva's hair was tidy. **(tidy/tousled)**
- Temperatures stay the same throughout the year. **(stay the same/fluctuate)**
- The victorious team lost to its opponent. **(lost to/overwhelmed)**

❹ Read each sentence and ask students to decide if it is true or false. If the sentence is false, instruct students to explain why.

- Very short hair is very rarely tousled. **(true)**
- Healthy people's temperatures don't fluctuate much. **(true)**
- *Overwhelmed* and *overpowered* are synonyms. **(true)**
- We perceive sounds by reading about them. **(false; we perceive sounds with our sense of hearing)**

Answers for page 131: 1. D, 2. G, 3. C, 4. J

Name _____

Week 32
A Word a Day

Review Words   tousled • perceive • overwhelmed • fluctuate

Fill in the bubble next to the correct answer.

1. Which word is a synonym for *fluctuate*?
   - Ⓐ stall
   - Ⓑ begin
   - Ⓒ conclude
   - Ⓓ change

2. Which person is most likely to feel *overwhelmed*?
   - Ⓕ Jim, whose summer vacation starts today
   - Ⓖ Jill, who has a huge project to complete
   - Ⓗ Joe, who is walking his dog in the park
   - Ⓙ Jen, who is sleeping late on a Saturday

3. Which might be *tousled*?
   - Ⓐ a freshly ironed shirt
   - Ⓑ dishes and silverware
   - Ⓒ sheets on which you tossed and turned all night
   - Ⓓ books shelved in a neat row

4. Which do you use to *perceive* things?
   - Ⓕ your senses of smell and taste
   - Ⓖ your hearing and eyesight
   - Ⓗ your sense of touch
   - Ⓙ all five of your senses

Writing

Write about a place where you love to go. Describe how that place looks, sounds, smells, and feels. Use **perceive** in your sentences.

_____

_____

_____

Week 33
A Word a Day

artifact

noun

a man-made object from the past

> The museum was filled with pottery, weapons, and other **artifacts** from early civilizations.

Which of these could be **artifacts**?

- a gold coin
- a new shoe
- a gum wrapper
- an ancient vase
- a Roman mosaic

What kind of **artifact** would you like to see or own?

congenial

adjective

having a pleasant personality

> The tour guide was both knowledgeable and **congenial**, making our time in San Francisco interesting and fun.

Which words mean about the same as **congenial**?

- good-natured
- grumpy
- negligent
- sociable
- outgoing

Name someone you know who is **congenial**. Describe the person's **congenial** behavior.

Week 33
A Word a Day

mutter

verb

to speak in a low, unclear way, barely moving the lips

We lose points on our oral reports if we **mutter** when we speak.

Complete this graphic organizer for **mutter**.

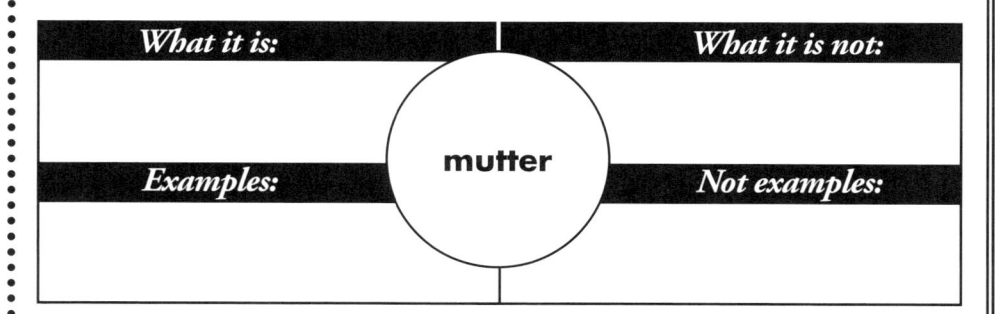

What it is:	What it is not:
Examples:	Not examples:

(center: mutter)

Mutter something to your neighbor. Now say it again clearly.

metamorphosis

noun

a complete change in form, appearance, or character

After its **metamorphosis**, a caterpillar becomes a butterfly.

Which words mean about the same as **metamorphosis**?

- change
- stability
- endurance
- consistency
- transformation

Describe another animal that experiences **metamorphosis**.

Review

Week 33
A Word a Day

artifact • congenial • mutter • metamorphosis

Write on the board the four words studied this week. Read the words with the class and briefly review their meanings. Then conduct the oral activities below.

1 Tell students that you are going to give them a clue about one of the words for the week. They are to find the word that answers the clue.

- A frog has gone through one. **(a metamorphosis)**
- You do this when you don't want people to understand what you're saying. **(mutter)**
- This word describes a good host. **(congenial)**
- This is an object made by humans that might be as much as a thousand years old. **(an artifact)**

2 Read each sentence and ask students to supply the correct word to complete the sentence.

- This sculpture is an ___ from an ancient civilization. **(artifact)**
- The changes in communication brought about by the Internet could be called a kind of ___. **(metamorphosis)**
- "What an idiot," I ___. Luckily, no one hears me. **(mutter)**
- It isn't ___ to frown at other people. **(congenial)**

3 Read each sentence and ask students to tell which word or words are wrong. Then have them provide the correct word from the week's list.

- Professor Mudrick dug up some modern tools that the ancient Romans used. **(modern tools/artifacts)**
- I can never understand John, because he speaks so clearly. **(speaks so clearly/mutters)**
- Our unfriendly host made us feel right at home. **(unfriendly/congenial)**

4 Read each sentence and ask students to decide if it is true or false. If the sentence is false, instruct students to explain why.

- A mealworm undergoes a metamorphosis to become a beetle. **(true)**
- A brand-new necklace is an artifact. **(false; an artifact is something from the past)**
- *Mutter* and *shout* are synonyms. **(false; they are antonyms)**
- Congenial people are polite to others. **(true)**

Answers for page 135: 1. A, 2. G, 3. D, 4. H

Name _____

Week 33
A Word a Day

Review Words: artifact • congenial • mutter • metamorphosis

Fill in the bubble next to the correct answer.

1. Which word is a synonym for *congenial*?
   - Ⓐ friendly
   - Ⓑ grumpy
   - Ⓒ distracted
   - Ⓓ proud

2. Which sentence describes a *metamorphosis*?
   - Ⓕ I recognized Jill as soon as I saw her, as she hadn't changed a bit.
   - Ⓖ As a kitten, Jack was small and delicate, but now he's enormous.
   - Ⓗ The library looks much the same as it did when it was built in 1950.
   - Ⓙ Hiking up the mountain, I recognized some familiar rock formations.

3. Where would you be most likely to see an *artifact*?
   - Ⓐ under your bed
   - Ⓑ on a grocery store shelf
   - Ⓒ in your refrigerator
   - Ⓓ in a museum display

4. How is a listener likely to respond when someone *mutters*?
   - Ⓕ "Please speak more softly—you're hurting my ears!"
   - Ⓖ "Don't be so rude—it hurts my feelings!"
   - Ⓗ "Please speak up, I can't understand you."
   - Ⓙ "What a beautiful singing voice you have!"

Writing

Write about a time when a metamorphosis surprised you. Use **metamorphosis** in your sentences.

_____
_____
_____

© Evan-Moor Corp. • EMC 2795 • A Word a Day   **135**

Week 34
A Word a Day

tumultuous

adjective

full of upheaval; wild and chaotic

There was a **tumultuous** sea battle between the pirate ships.

Complete this graphic organizer for **tumultuous**.

Examples: — **tumultuous** — *Other Ways to Say It:*

Give an example of a **tumultuous** period in history.

query

noun

a question

verb

to raise a question

The teacher wrote a **query** in the margin of my paper. She **queried** me about the dates I had included.

Which meaning is being used: "a question" or "to raise a question"?

- I will respond to your query once I have all the facts.
- My teacher uses her red pen to query anything that is unclear in my writing.
- My excuse for being late caused Ramona to query my actual whereabouts.
- The journalist queried the politician about his plans to run for president.
- The criminal tried to avoid answering the judge's query.

Give an example of a **query** you would like answered.

Week 34
A Word a Day

diagnosis

noun

a medical opinion given after studying a patient's symptoms

According to the doctor's **diagnosis**, my injured ankle would heal in three months.

Which words mean about the same as **diagnosis**?

- judgment
- guess
- conclusion
- query
- finding

What types of symptoms and procedures would lead to the **diagnosis** of a broken ankle?

jaunty

adjective

displaying a carefree, self-confident manner

It was obvious from his **jaunty** walk that he was feeling good about the day's events.

Which words mean about the same as **jaunty**?

- happy-go-lucky
- overwhelmed
- lighthearted
- sprightly
- gloomy

Give an example of an occasion when you felt **jaunty**.

Review

Week 34
A Word a Day

tumultuous • query • diagnosis • jaunty

Write on the board the four words studied this week. Read the words with the class and briefly review their meanings. Then conduct the oral activities below.

❶ Tell students that you are going to give them a clue about one of the words for the week. They are to find the word that answers the clue.

- This ends with a question mark. **(a query)**

- A doctor makes one before prescribing medicine. **(a diagnosis)**

- This word describes how you might feel in a stylish outfit. **(jaunty)**

- If two friends quarrel constantly, this word might describe their friendship. **(tumultuous)**

❷ Read each sentence and ask students to supply the correct word to complete the sentence.

- It is an editor's job to _____ parts of an author's work that seem unclear. **(query)**

- My symptoms were so odd that it was difficult for my doctor to make a _____. **(diagnosis)**

- Joaquin wore his cap at a _____ angle. **(jaunty)**

- The Civil War years were _____ for both soldiers and civilians. **(tumultuous)**

❸ Read each sentence and ask students to tell which word or words are wrong. Then have them provide the correct word from the week's list.

- The Civil War period was a peaceful era in U.S. history. **(peaceful/tumultuous)**

- I have an answer: What is your middle name? **(an answer/a query)**

- His sluggish step gave away his cheerful mood. **(sluggish/jaunty)**

❹ Read each sentence and ask students to decide if it is true or false. If the sentence is false, instruct students to explain why.

- A doctor treats a patient's illness before making a diagnosis. **(false; a diagnosis is made before treatment)**

- A hurricane is one example of tumultuous weather. **(true)**

- *Query* and *reply* are synonyms. **(false; they are antonyms)**

- Students probably have a jaunty appearance when school is dismissed for vacation. **(true)**

Answers for page 139: 1. D, 2. H, 3. C, 4. F

Week 34
A Word a Day

Name _____

Review Words tumultuous • query • diagnosis • jaunty

Fill in the bubble next to the correct answer.

1. Which word is a synonym for *jaunty*?
   - Ⓐ useful
   - Ⓑ boring
   - Ⓒ downhearted
   - Ⓓ cheerful

2. Which sentence is a *query*?
   - Ⓕ Please stack your dirty dishes in the sink.
   - Ⓖ What a terrible mess you've made!
   - Ⓗ Have you finished eating breakfast?
   - Ⓙ I love waffles, pancakes, and French toast.

3. Who is qualified to make a medical *diagnosis*?
   - Ⓐ a criminal lawyer
   - Ⓑ a fifth-grade teacher
   - Ⓒ a children's doctor
   - Ⓓ a bank teller

4. Which word is an antonym for *tumultuous*?
   - Ⓕ calm
   - Ⓖ stormy
   - Ⓗ tense
   - Ⓙ terrific

Writing

Think of a person who interests you. Write some questions for him or her. Use **query** or **queries** in your sentences.

_____
_____
_____

© Evan-Moor Corp. • EMC 2795 • A Word a Day

Week 35
A Word a Day

wriggle

verb

to squirm

We watched the snake **wriggle** as it worked to shed its old skin.

Complete this graphic organizer for **wriggle**.

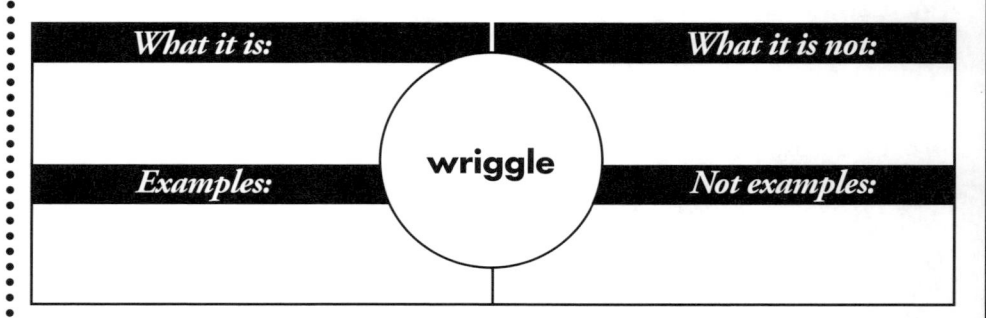

What it is:		What it is not:
	wriggle	
Examples:		Not examples:

What is something that makes you **wriggle**?

corrupt

adjective

dishonestly using your position to your advantage, especially for money

A **corrupt** official at city hall accepted money to get his friend's parking tickets taken off the records.

Which words mean about the same as **corrupt**?

- loyal
- crooked
- unprincipled
- immoral
- law-abiding

What examples of **corrupt** actions have you heard about in the news?

Week 35
A Word a Day

uncouth

adjective

lacking in manners; rough and rude

Uncouth people are seldom invited to dinner a second time.

Which of these are examples of **uncouth** behavior?
- showing up at a party when you weren't invited
- burping at the table
- wiping your mouth on your sleeve
- taking small bites and chewing quietly
- shoving your way to the front of the line

In what type of setting would it be inappropriate to behave in an **uncouth** manner?

aspire

verb

to want or try very hard to achieve a goal

When I grow up, I **aspire** to become a doctor.

Which of these might people **aspire** to become?
- an actor or actress
- a college graduate
- a criminal
- a parent
- an infant

What is something that you **aspire** to?

Review

Week 35
A Word a Day

wriggle • corrupt • uncouth • aspire

Write on the board the four words studied this week. Read the words with the class and briefly review their meanings. Then conduct the oral activities below.

❶ Tell students that you are going to give them a clue about one of the words for the week. They are to find the word that answers the clue.

- Someone could go to jail for this kind of act. **(corrupt)**
- You do this when you try to reach a goal. **(aspire to it)**
- Snakes and worms do this. **(wriggle)**
- This word describes someone with bad manners. **(uncouth)**

❷ Read each sentence and ask students to supply the correct word to complete the sentence.

- My ___ behavior was due to not being used to eating in fancy restaurants. **(uncouth)**
- The two-year-old tried to ___ out of her father's arms. **(wriggle)**
- I ___ to become an architect after I finish college. **(aspire)**
- City residents voted to fire the ___ mayor, who gave jobs to his friends and family. **(corrupt)**

❸ Read each sentence and ask students to tell which word or words are wrong. Then have them provide the correct word from the week's list.

- Snakes walk across the hot desert sand. **(walk/wriggle)**
- "Huh?" is a polite way to ask, "Pardon me?" **(a polite/an uncouth)**
- A president who is known for being honest is unlikely to be reelected. **(honest/corrupt)**

❹ Read each sentence and ask students to decide if it is true or false. If the sentence is false, instruct students to explain why.

- Few students aspire to do well in school. **(false; most students want to do well)**
- It is appropriate to behave in an uncouth manner at a fancy party. **(false; it's inappropriate)**
- Wriggling is similar to stomping. **(false; it is similar to wiggling and slithering)**
- An official who steals public money is corrupt. **(true)**

Answers for page 143: 1. D, 2. J, 3. B, 4. F

Name _____

Week 35
A Word a Day

Review Words wriggle • corrupt • uncouth • aspire

Fill in the bubble next to the correct answer.

1. **Which phrase means the opposite of *uncouth*?**
   - Ⓐ well-done
   - Ⓑ well-prepared
   - Ⓒ well-fed
   - Ⓓ well-mannered

2. **Which word is a synonym for *wriggle*?**
   - Ⓕ gallop
   - Ⓖ patter
   - Ⓗ stomp
   - Ⓙ squirm

3. **What do people do when they *aspire* to goals?**
   - Ⓐ They finally achieve them.
   - Ⓑ They try hard to reach them.
   - Ⓒ They fail to reach them.
   - Ⓓ They lose interest in them.

4. **In which sentence is *corrupt* used correctly?**
   - Ⓕ Let's vote for an honest candidate with no history of being corrupt.
   - Ⓖ I admire the mayor for being corrupt. He always says exactly what he thinks.
   - Ⓗ Be corrupt, get good grades, and work hard, and you'll get into college.
   - Ⓙ Because the senator was corrupt, we gave her large donations.

Writing

Write about someone you know who aspires to a goal. Use **aspire** in your sentences.

_____
_____
_____

© Evan-Moor Corp. • EMC 2795 • A Word a Day

Week 36
A Word a Day

timber

noun

wood used in building things

synonym: lumber

> The **timber** used to build our house came from Pennsylvania.

Which of the following could be constructed from **timber**?

- a skyscraper
- a treehouse
- a doghouse
- a submarine
- a mountain cabin

Give some examples of things that are made from **timber**.

mundane

adjective

practical or ordinary

> After my vacation in Hawaii, staying at home seemed very **mundane**.

Which words mean about the same as **mundane**?

- exceptional
- everyday
- normal
- special
- usual

What is a **mundane** weekend like for you?

Week 36
A Word a Day

compile

verb

to put together in a list or volume

We had to compile all our stories into a class reader.

Complete this graphic organizer for **compile**.

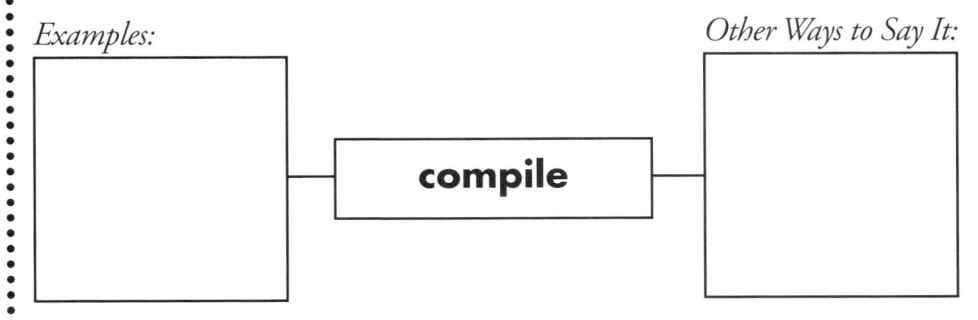

Examples: — compile — *Other Ways to Say It:*

What kind of list could you **compile** to help yourself be more organized?

quintessential

adjective

the most typical example of something; the essence

The Egyptian pyramids are quintessential examples of geometry in architecture.

Which words mean about the same as **quintessential**?

- fundamental
- essential
- unusual
- primary
- atypical

What do you think is the **quintessential** characteristic of a successful person?

Review

Week 36
A Word a Day

timber • mundane • compile • quintessential

Write on the board the four words studied this week. Read the words with the class and briefly review their meanings. Then conduct the oral activities below.

❶ Tell students that you are going to give them a clue about one of the words for the week. They are to find the word that answers the clue.

- You do this when you gather a list of names. **(compile them)**
- This word describes an everyday chore like making your bed. **(mundane)**
- This is a building material. **(timber)**
- This word describes a typical example. **(quintessential)**

❷ Read each sentence and ask students to supply the correct word to complete the sentence.

- The *Batman* movies are ___ examples of action films. **(quintessential)**
- Dad claims to enjoy ___ tasks such as washing the dishes. **(mundane)**
- The lumber mill cuts logs into ___ for builders. **(timber)**
- Ms. McIlvaine plans to ___ our poems in an illustrated poetry book. **(compile)**

❸ Read each sentence and ask students to tell which word or words are wrong. Then have them provide the correct word from the week's list.

- Vanilla ice cream is an odd example of a simple dessert. **(an odd/a quintessential)**
- The bricks for this wooden house came from an Oregon forest. **(bricks/timber)**
- Setting the table is the most exciting job I can imagine. **(exciting/mundane)**

❹ Read each sentence and ask students to decide if it is true or false. If the sentence is false, instruct students to explain why.

- To compile stories means to put them together in a book. **(true)**
- A quintessential example is as typical as can be. **(true)**
- *Timber* and *lumber* are synonyms. **(true)**
- Most people think that acting in movies is a mundane job. **(false; most people think it is a glamorous, unusual job)**

Answers for page 147: 1. C, 2. J, 3. B, 4. G

Name _____

Week 36
A Word a Day

Review Words   timber • mundane • compile • quintessential

Fill in the bubble next to the correct answer.

1. Which word is an antonym for *quintessential*?
   - Ⓐ unfinished
   - Ⓑ uncomfortable
   - Ⓒ nonstandard
   - Ⓓ unimpressive

2. Which word is a synonym for *timber*?
   - Ⓕ plaster
   - Ⓖ steel
   - Ⓗ brick
   - Ⓙ wood

3. Which is a *mundane* job or chore?
   - Ⓐ piloting a spaceship
   - Ⓑ taking out the garbage
   - Ⓒ taming a wild grizzly bear
   - Ⓓ writing a best-selling book

4. Which of these might someone *compile*?
   - Ⓕ dried autumn leaves
   - Ⓖ recipes for a cookbook
   - Ⓗ weapons for an army
   - Ⓙ pillows on a sofa

Writing

Write about an ordinary chore that you don't mind doing. Explain why you don't mind doing that chore. Use **mundane** in your sentences.

_____

_____

_____

Dictionary

abominable • belfry

Aa

abominable • *adjective*
something hideous and unappealing
synonym: disgusting
As we approached the garbage dump, the abominable odor nearly knocked me out!

amateur • *noun*
a person who does something for pleasure, not for pay
If you excel in a sport as an amateur, you may be good enough to get paid to do it as a professional athlete.

ancestor • *noun*
a member of your family who lived a long time ago, even before your grandparents
I have an ancestor who fought in the American Civil War.

annex
verb
to add or attach to something larger
noun
a wing added to a building
The hospital had to annex a building next door when it opened the new pediatric annex.

antidote • *noun*
something that works against the effects of poison
People bitten by poisonous snakes need to be given an antidote as soon as possible to prevent serious illness or death.

appease • *verb*
to make calmer by giving in to demands
synonym: satisfy
The band came back on stage and played another song to appease its screaming fans.

aptitude • *noun*
a natural ability or talent
Lucita has an excellent sense of color and shows a strong aptitude for painting.

artifact • *noun*
a man-made object from the past
The museum was filled with pottery, weapons, and other artifacts from early civilizations.

aspire • *verb*
to want or try very hard to achieve a goal
When I grow up, I aspire to become a doctor.

asset • *noun*
something valuable or useful
Her great speed combined with endurance was a wonderful asset to the track team.

automatic • *adjective*
operating without a person's control
In the past, we had to pour water in trays and freeze it to make ice, but now we have a new refrigerator with an automatic ice maker.

Bb

balmy • *adjective*
soothing and mild
The balmy spring weather felt refreshing after the long winter.

bask • *verb*
to lie in and enjoy a warm place
On warm spring days, my cat loves to sit on the windowsill and bask in the sun.

belfry • *noun*
a tower where bells are hung
The bell ringer climbed the winding staircase to the belfry every evening at 5:00 to ring the hour.

blotch • coy

blotch • *noun*
a large spot or stain
The grape juice left a dark blotch on the white carpet.

brawny • *adjective*
muscular and strong
synonym: powerful
The brawny lumberjack easily sawed through the logs.

Cc

chronic • *adjective*
1. lasting a long time; occurring repeatedly
2. done by habit

My grandma has chronic arthritis pain. Instead of being a chronic complainer, she uses pain medication.

collate • *verb*
to put pages together in the correct order
When the pages of my report got mixed up, I had to collate them.

compile • *verb*
to put together in a list or volume
We had to compile all our stories into a class reader.

condemn • *verb*
to express strong disapproval
Our school condemns all bullying.

condense • *verb*
1. to change from a gas to a liquid
2. to make shorter or more concise

My report on how water vapor in the air condenses to make rain is too lengthy. My teacher said I must condense it to two pages.

congenial • *adjective*
having a pleasant personality
The tour guide was both knowledgeable and congenial, making our time in San Francisco interesting and fun.

congested • *adjective*
1. to be overcrowded or filled to overflowing
2. having too much mucus in a body part

We drove to the pharmacy to get medicine for my congested sinuses. It took a long time because it was rush hour and the streets were congested with traffic.

contemporary • *adjective*
up-to-date; modern or current
antonym: old
The contemporary digital clock looked out of place among the antique furnishings.

contribute • *verb*
to give help or money
The women's organization was able to contribute ten thousand dollars for restoring the old schoolhouse.

convertible
noun
an automobile with a top that can be folded back or removed
adjective
able to be changed
Even with the top down on the convertible, we couldn't fit the convertible sofa bed in the car.

correspond • *verb*
1. to communicate in writing
2. to match in some way

When you correspond with someone in Japan, you have to write the Japanese pictographs that correspond to that person's address.

corrupt • *adjective*
dishonestly using your position to your advantage, especially for money
A corrupt official at city hall accepted money to get his friend's parking tickets taken off the records.

coy • *adjective*
shy or bashful
The coy child hid behind her mother when a stranger came to the door.

© Evan-Moor Corp. • EMC 2795 • A Word a Day

critique • extravagant

critique • *verb*
to give an opinion of the positive and negative points of something
Before I write my final story draft, I will ask some classmates to critique my rough draft to get ideas for ways to improve the plot.

curfew • *noun*
a rule that prevents people from moving around freely after dark
Our community has an eleven o'clock curfew for people under sixteen years old.

Dd

denominator • *noun*
the number below the line in a fraction
In a fraction, the denominator indicates the number of parts a whole number is divided into.

deplete • *verb*
to use up
Buying those expensive basketball shoes will deplete my savings.

diagnosis • *noun*
a medical opinion given after studying a patient's symptoms
According to the doctor's diagnosis, my injured ankle would heal in three months.

dimension • *noun*
a measurement of length, width, or thickness
We need to figure out the room's dimensions so we can buy the right amount of paint.

disheveled • *adjective*
untidy; rumpled
After my brother and I finished a bedtime pillow fight, both of our beds were disheveled.

domestic • *adjective*
1. related to the home or family
2. tame; not wild
Although I enjoy most domestic activities, I hate cleaning up after our domestic ferret.

dominate • *verb*
to rule or control by strength or power
The king used his soldiers to help him dominate the kingdom.

dormant • *adjective*
not active; sleeping
The volcano has been dormant for hundreds of years.

Ee

elevate • *verb*
to raise or lift up
The mechanic had to elevate the car in order to have room to work underneath it.

emancipate • *verb*
to set free from slavery or control
President Lincoln helped to emancipate the slaves in the South.

emotion • *noun*
any strong feeling
The new father was overcome with emotion as he gazed at his infant daughter.

endurance • *noun*
the ability to withstand stress or hardship
The marathon runner has the endurance to run thirty miles.

exquisite • *adjective*
of exceptional beauty; finely made
The exquisite embroidery must have taken hours to complete.

extravagant • *adjective*
spending lots of money in a free and careless way
He was extravagant in his purchase of expensive gifts for his friends.

Ff

facilitate • *verb*
to make less difficult; to help to progress
The outdoor drop box facilitates the return of library materials.

falsehood • *noun*
a lie or an untruth
antonym: truth
Sheila's claim that she met a movie star when she visited Los Angeles turned out to be a falsehood. She merely saw a famous actor in a restaurant.

flammable • *adjective*
easily set on fire
The rags soaked in gasoline were extremely flammable.

flourish • *verb*
to grow or develop in a strong and healthy way
We hope our tomato plants will flourish in the rich soil.

fluctuate • *verb*
to shift back and forth uncertainly
The weather seemed to fluctuate daily, which made it hard to schedule the beach party.

friction • *noun*
disagreement between people or groups of people
There was friction between the two teams when a wild pitch injured the batter.

Gg

garland • *noun*
a ring of flowers or leaves; a wreath
A beautiful garland made of holly was used to decorate our front door.

glutton • *noun*
someone who eats and drinks greedily
An all-you-can-eat restaurant is the perfect place for a glutton.

gratify • *verb*
to give pleasure or satisfaction
Angela's good grades in school will gratify her parents.

Hh

harmonious • *adjective*
being in agreement; peaceful
After the argument was settled, a harmonious feeling returned to the class.

hearty • *adjective*
full of warmth and friendliness
My grandfather gave us a hearty welcome when we arrived.

horde • *noun*
a large, moving crowd
synonym: swarm
A horde of spectators rushed from the stadium after the powerful earthquake.

humble • *adjective*
1. not proud; modest
2. simple; not fancy
The humble artist refused to take large sums of money for his beautiful paintings. He lived simply in a humble studio outside the city.

humorous • *adjective*
full of humor; amusing
synonym: funny
People laughed all evening as they enjoyed the humorous play.

Ii

immaculate • *adjective*

extremely clean and neat

I've spent all morning cleaning my bedroom, and now it is immaculate.

immerse • *verb*

1. to involve or occupy completely
2. to cover completely with water or liquid

She was so immersed in the magazine she was reading that she immersed her sleeve in her bowl of soup.

impartial • *adjective*

not favoring one over the other

synonym: fair

It was hard for the referee to be impartial when his son's team was playing.

implore • *verb*

to beg urgently

synonym: plead

It doesn't matter how much we implore—our mother never lets us rent PG-13 movies.

indication • *noun*

something that points out or indicates; a sign

The smiling faces were a good indication that everyone was having a good time.

inundate • *verb*

1. to flood or overflow
2. to overrun or overwhelm

The heavy rains caused the river to rise and inundate the lowlands. The nearby fields were inundated with ants fleeing from the rising water.

invincible • *adjective*

not able to be defeated

With five victories and no defeats, our team has been invincible this season.

Jj

jaunty • *adjective*

displaying a carefree, self-confident manner

It was obvious from his jaunty walk that he was feeling good about the day's events.

jostled • *verb*

bumped or pushed around roughly

The passengers were jostled about when the train came to a sudden stop.

junction • *noun*

a place where things meet or cross

We live at the junction of Main Street and Maple Avenue.

jut • *verb*

to stick out sharply

The ocean scenery along this part of the coast is made more interesting by rocks that jut out of the water.

Kk

killjoy • *noun*

a person who spoils the fun of others

Marcy was a killjoy when she insisted on telling us how fattening and unhealthful the chocolate dessert was.

kindling • *noun*

dried twigs or small pieces of wood used to start a fire

The boys had to search the ground for kindling before they could build a campfire.

knoll • *noun*

a small, rounded hill

We climbed to the top of the knoll to get a clear view of the sunset.

lapse • overwhelmed

Ll

lapse
noun
1. a small mistake or failure
2. the passing of time
Forgive my lapse of good table manners, but it's been a two-year lapse since I've eaten in a fancy restaurant.

leisure • *noun*
freedom from work or other duties; free time
When I get home from work, I spend much of my leisure time playing with my dogs.

loathe • *verb*
to dislike greatly
antonym: adore
I loathe running around the track after it rains, because I always get covered with mud.

loiter • *verb*
to stand around in a public place doing nothing in particular
The shopping center is locked up at night to prevent loitering.

Mm

metamorphosis • *noun*
a complete change in form, appearance, or character
After its metamorphosis, a caterpillar becomes a butterfly.

mundane • *adjective*
practical or ordinary
After my vacation in Hawaii, staying at home seemed very mundane.

muse • *verb*
to think deeply
My mother had to muse for a while before deciding to let me have a slumber party.

mutter • *verb*
to speak in a low, unclear way, barely moving the lips
We lose points on our oral reports if we mutter when we speak.

Nn

native • *noun*
a person born or raised in a particular place
My grandmother is a native of the Philippines, and she returns there every year.

navigate • *verb*
to steer or direct the course of a ship or an aircraft
To navigate a ship in heavy fog is difficult because you can't see where the ship is headed.

negligent • *adjective*
not showing proper care or concern
Only a negligent pet owner would allow a dog to stay outside all day without water.

noxious • *adjective*
harmful to the health of living beings
They evacuated the workers from the factory after a noxious chemical spilled.

Oo

ovation • *noun*
a loud and enthusiastic show of approval
The audience gave the choir a standing ovation at the end of the concert.

overwhelmed
verb
overpowered or made helpless
adjective
burdened or loaded with an excess of something
Huge waves overwhelmed the boat. The sailors were overwhelmed with relief when the Coast Guard came to rescue them.

© Evan-Moor Corp. • EMC 2795 • A Word a Day

Pp

pandemonium • *noun*
a wild uproar
There was pandemonium in the stadium when the home team won the championship game.

paraphrase • *verb*
to use other words to explain something
The teacher asked us to paraphrase the story in fifty words or less.

partial • *adjective*
1. not complete
2. unfair favor to one side

My teacher will not accept partial homework assignments, even from the students she seems to be partial to.

pedigree • *noun*
a list of ancestors of a person or an animal
Our puppy was expensive because his pedigree includes several champion show dogs.

pell-mell • *adjective*
in a hasty, confused, and disorderly manner
The books were thrown pell-mell onto the shelf.

perceive • *verb*
to become aware of something by experiencing it through the senses
We could barely perceive the bird's song over the roar of the waterfall.

phenomenon • *noun*
1. a fact or an event that can be seen or felt
2. something unusual and remarkable

Lightning is a natural phenomenon that has always awed people.

The Beatles were a phenomenon that thrilled young people during the '60s.

ponder • *verb*
to think about something very carefully
You should take some time to ponder the question before writing your response.

procrastinate • *verb*
to put off doing something until a future time
I'd better start writing and not procrastinate any longer, because the report is due tomorrow.

prosperous • *adjective*
having economic well-being
synonym: wealthy
The prosperous business donated thousands of dollars so that a swimming pool could be built at the high school.

pulsate • *verb*
to beat in rhythm, as the heart does
On foggy nights, you can see the glow of the roller coaster's flashing neon lights pulsate through the mist.

pungent • *adjective*
sharp or strong to the senses of taste or smell
The pungent odor of fish could be smelled from one end of the wharf to the other.

Qq

quagmire • *noun*
1. soft, wet, soggy ground
2. a difficult situation; a predicament

When the trail led us to the edge of a quagmire, we were in a quagmire about how to get around the large, muddy area.

query
noun
a question
verb
to raise a question
The teacher wrote a query in the margin of my paper. She queried me about the dates I had included.

quintessential • tactful

quintessential • *adjective*

the most typical example of something; the essence

The Egyptian pyramids are quintessential examples of geometry in architecture.

Rr

radiate • *verb*

to give off heat or light

The heat that radiated from the campfire almost melted the soles of my sneakers.

ravenous • *adjective*

very hungry

The ravenous kittens all fought for a place at the saucer of milk.

rebellion • *noun*

a show of opposition to a form of authority

The Minutemen were an important part of the American colonials' rebellion against Britain.

recoil • *verb*

to draw back in fear or disgust

We saw the dog recoil as it came across a rattlesnake on the path.

remote • *adjective*

1. far away
2. small; slight

The cabin was in a remote location about 25 miles from the nearest town. There was a remote chance that visitors would drop by.

rendezvous

noun

a place for meeting

verb

to meet at a previously arranged time and place

The playground was a popular rendezvous for the girls on the basketball team. They planned to rendezvous there right after school.

retaliate • *verb*

to strike back; to get revenge

It's best to avoid a bully. You could get hurt if you try to retaliate.

rustic • *adjective*

having to do with the countryside, not the city

The rustic cabin looked out of place in the suburban neighborhood.

Ss

scuffle • *noun*

a confused struggle or fight

The argument became a scuffle when one boy grabbed the other's cap.

sincere • *adjective*

genuine; true

Cory's sincere apology made me feel better because I could tell he was truly sorry.

snob • *noun*

a person who feels he or she is better than others

Michael is such a snob. He's always bragging about his expensive clothes and toys.

Spartan • *adjective*

strictly self-disciplined; not easy or comfortable

The wrestler followed a Spartan routine in his training, working out three hours every day.

susceptible • *adjective*

easily influenced or affected

The medical assistant wore a surgical mask so she wouldn't be susceptible to catching colds.

Tt

tactful • *adjective*

thoughtful and sensitive in dealing with others

The tactful waiter quickly and quietly removed the glass of water with a fly in it.

taffeta • tumultuous

taffeta • *noun*
a stiff, crisp, shiny fabric made of silk, nylon, or rayon
The ballerina's tutu was made of beautiful lavender taffeta.

tamper • *verb*
to interfere with something so as to damage or change it
In some countries, it is common for candidates to tamper with the voting ballots in order to win an election.

tantalize • *verb*
to tease with something desirable but withhold it
It is cruel to tantalize caged animals with tempting foods.

tariff • *noun*
a tax paid on products that are imported or exported
On December 16, 1773, 150 American colonists dressed as Mohawk Indians dumped 342 crates of tea into Boston Harbor to protest a British tariff on tea.

tarnish • *verb*
to dull the shine of a metal surface by exposure to air
If left on the table, the silver candlesticks will tarnish and require polishing.

tattered • *adjective*
broken-down or worn-out
After years of use, the tattered leather sofa was finally replaced.

temptation • *noun*
something that tempts or attracts
It was so hot that I could not fight the temptation to jump into the cool water.

terminate • *verb*
to bring to an end
We had to terminate our bike ride when it began to rain heavily.

timber • *noun*
wood used in building things
synonym: lumber
The timber used to build our house came from Pennsylvania.

tolerate • *verb*
to put up with something
synonym: endure
When my dog could no longer tolerate the kitten's playful nibbling, he turned around and barked at her.

tousled • *adjective*
in a tangled mass
Her hair was tousled after riding in the convertible.

tragedy • *noun*
1. an unfortunate or sad event
2. a play, movie, or story with a terribly sad ending

The sinking of the ocean liner Titanic *was a terrible tragedy. It cost millions of dollars to film the tragedy* Titanic, *which was a huge hit.*

translucent • *adjective*
allowing only some light to pass through so that images can't be seen clearly
Most bathroom windows are translucent to ensure privacy, but let some light in.

tuition • *noun*
money paid to attend a school or college
My sister is saving all the money from her summer job for college tuition.

tumultuous • *adjective*
full of upheaval; wild and chaotic
There was a tumultuous sea battle between the pirate ships.

Uu

uncouth • *adjective*
lacking in manners; rough and rude
Uncouth people are seldom invited to dinner a second time.

undaunted • *adjective*
not discouraged; not hesitating because of danger or difficulties
The hiker's hopes for rescue remained undaunted, even though he had been lost in the wilderness for two days.

undeniable • *adjective*
unquestionably true
After the fierce blizzard, it was undeniable that winter had truly arrived.

urge
verb
to speak or argue strongly in favor of
noun
a strong desire
The basketball coach had to urge her star player to control the urge to take wild shots.

Vv

versatile • *adjective*
able to do many different things well
Raul is a versatile athlete who can run, throw, and kick very well.

vertical • *adjective*
straight up and down
The first hill on the roller coaster ride was nearly vertical.

vicinity • *noun*
the area nearby
There are three playgrounds in the vicinity of my home.

vigorous • *adjective*
energetic, lively, and full of strength
We played a vigorous game of kickball at recess.

vital • *adjective*
necessary for supporting life
antonym: unimportant
Clean air is vital to human survival.

vulnerable • *adjective*
capable of being harmed or injured
Without its mother, the baby bird was vulnerable on the ground.

Ww

whimsical • *adjective*
odd or playful
synonym: fanciful
We had to smile at the whimsical calendar photographs of dogs wearing clothing.

wriggle • *verb*
to squirm
We watched the snake wriggle as it worked to shed its old skin.

Yy

yearn • *verb*
to have a strong wish or longing for something
After she moved to a new school, Margo missed her old friends and yearned to see them again.

Examples: *Other Ways to Say It:*

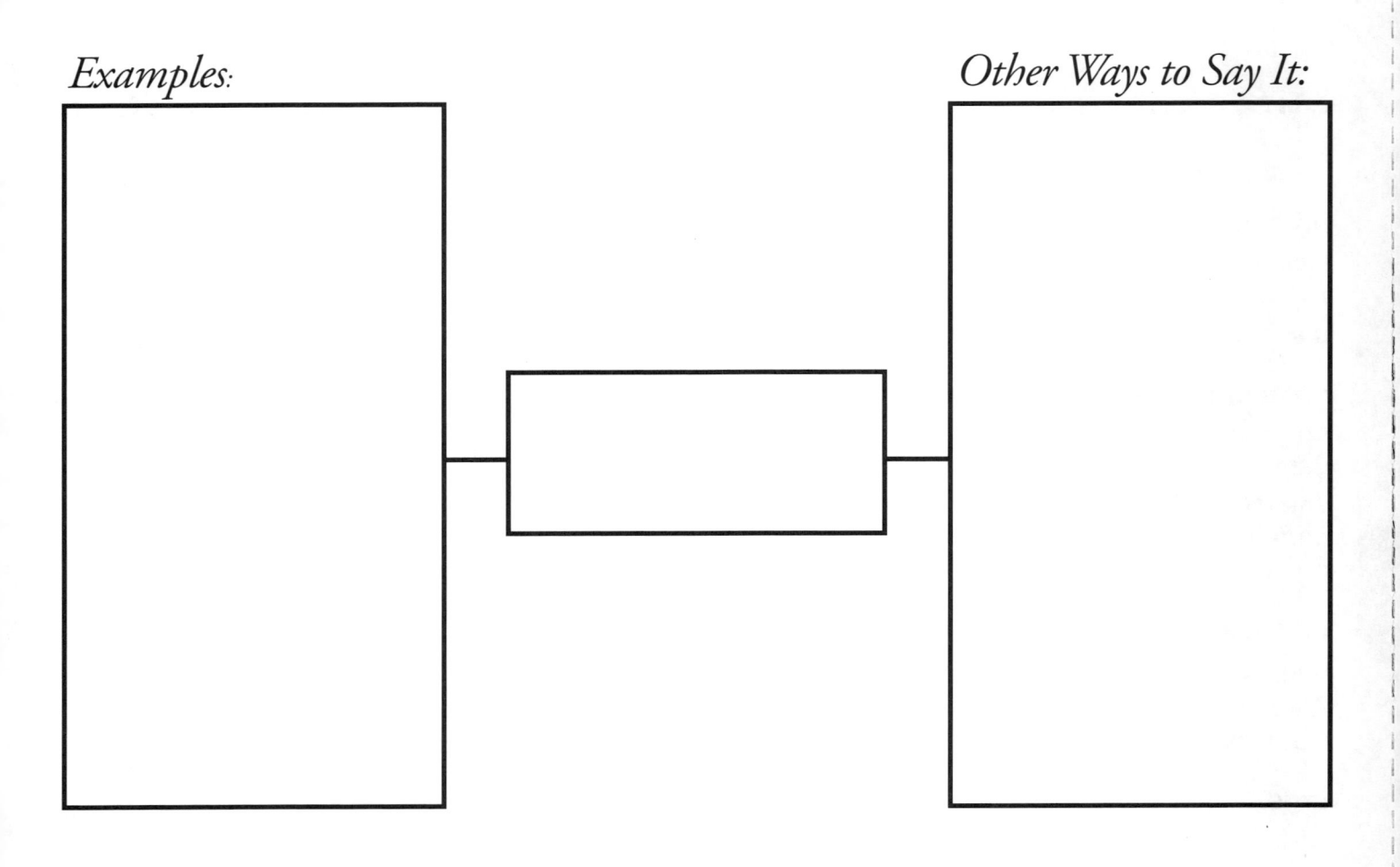

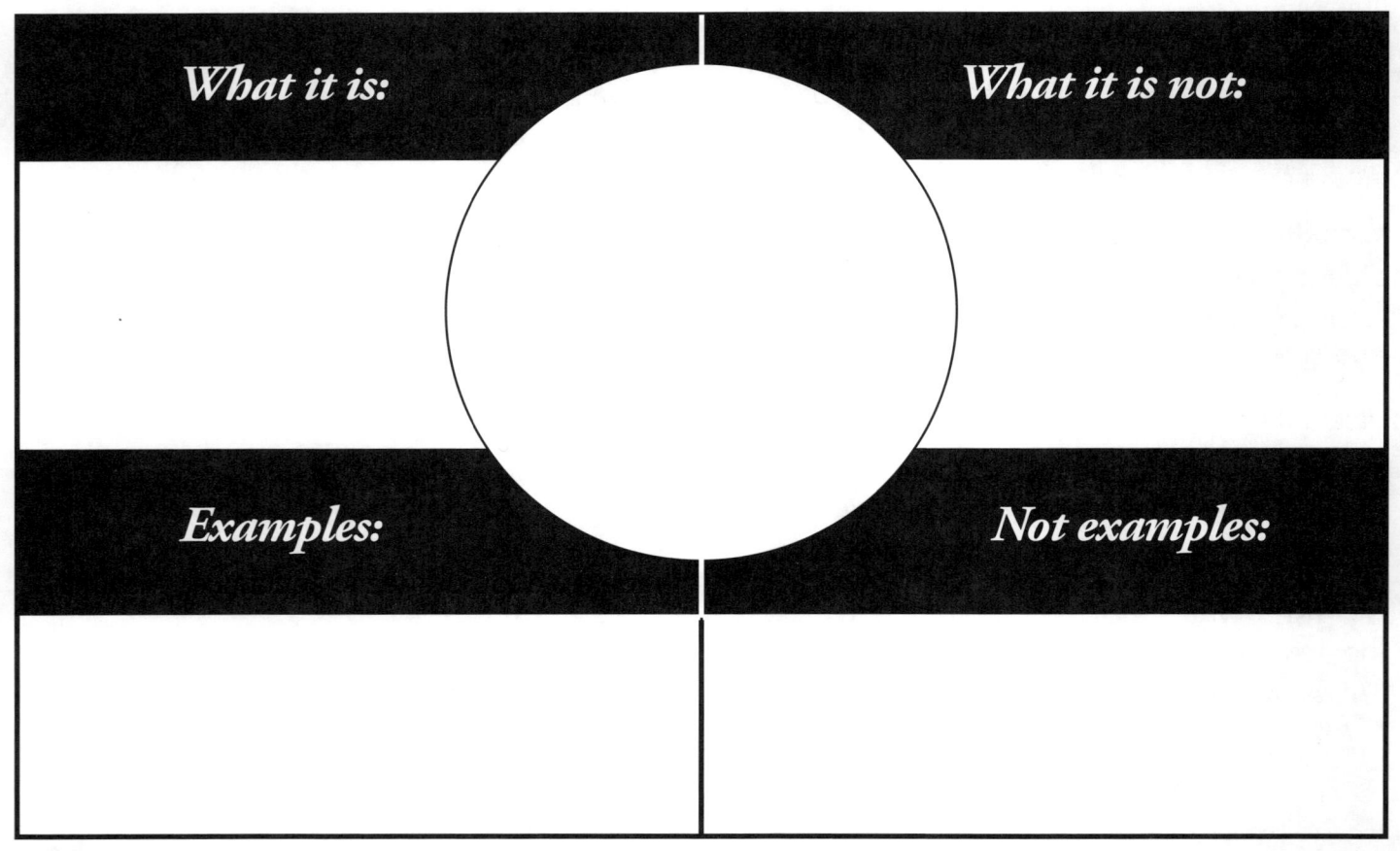

What it is: *What it is not:*

Examples: *Not examples:*

Index

abominable 105	domestic 41	knoll 33	retaliate 116
amateur 36	dominate 49	lapse 44	rustic 44
ancestor....... 48	dormant 124	leisure 113	scuffle 77
annex......... 81	elevate 4	loathe......... 61	sincere........ 61
antidote 100	emancipate 72	loiter.......... 100	snob.......... 16
appease....... 37	emotion 93	metamorphosis . 133	Spartan 104
aptitude 65	endurance 88	mundane 144	susceptible..... 73
artifact 132	exquisite....... 101	muse 52	tactful......... 56
aspire......... 141	extravagant 125	mutter 133	taffeta......... 96
asset 117	facilitate 121	native 105	tamper 12
automatic...... 17	falsehood...... 40	navigate 40	tantalize 80
balmy......... 68	flammable 5	negligent 76	tariff 53
bask.......... 68	flourish........ 13	noxious 25	tarnish 73
belfry 57	fluctuate....... 129	ovation........ 72	tattered 101
blotch......... 17	friction 60	overwhelmed ... 129	temptation 120
brawny 84	garland........ 4	pandemonium .. 108	terminate 109
chronic........ 113	glutton 20	paraphrase..... 52	timber......... 144
collate 9	gratify......... 32	partial......... 37	tolerate........ 33
compile 145	harmonious 21	pedigree....... 112	tousled........ 128
condemn 112	hearty 92	pell-mell 76	tragedy........ 64
condense...... 124	horde 5	perceive 128	translucent..... 116
congenial...... 132	humble........ 60	phenomenon ... 89	tuition......... 12
congested 16	humorous...... 97	ponder 24	tumultuous..... 136
contemporary... 80	immaculate 8	procrastinate ... 93	uncouth 141
contribute...... 97	immerse....... 120	prosperous..... 85	undaunted 65
convertible..... 29	impartial....... 32	pulsate........ 64	undeniable..... 77
correspond..... 45	implore........ 20	pungent 109	urge 56
corrupt 140	indication 96	quagmire 25	versatile 29
coy........... 45	inundate....... 88	query 136	vertical......... 69
critique........ 57	invincible 49	quintessential... 145	vicinity 81
curfew 84	jaunty......... 137	radiate 85	vigorous....... 13
denominator.... 69	jostled 92	ravenous 121	vital........... 89
deplete........ 21	junction 8	rebellion....... 36	vulnerable 53
diagnosis 137	jut............ 117	recoil 104	whimsical...... 28
dimension 48	killjoy 28	remote 125	wriggle 140
disheveled 108	kindling 41	rendezvous 24	yearn 9

© Evan-Moor Corp. • EMC 2795 • A Word a Day

159

Important vocabulary your students need to perform well in the classroom and on assessments!

Daily Academic Vocabulary

Provide your students with the important academic vocabulary practice and instruction they need to perform well in the classroom and on assessments! This research-based series contains 36 weeks of systematic vocabulary instruction supported by transparencies, teacher pages, student pages for each day, and weekly reviews. 160 reproducible pages *plus* 32 transparencies. ***Correlated to state standards.***

Daily Academic Vocabulary...

- *covers the key vocabulary words that students encounter in many different academic contexts, and*
- *uses speaking, listening, reading, and writing activities to engage students in vocabulary practice.*

Grade 2	EMC 2758-PRO	Grade 5	EMC 2761-PRO
Grade 3	EMC 2759-PRO	Grade 6+	EMC 2762-PRO
Grade 4	EMC 2760-PRO		

Research-Based

Ten-Minute Activities

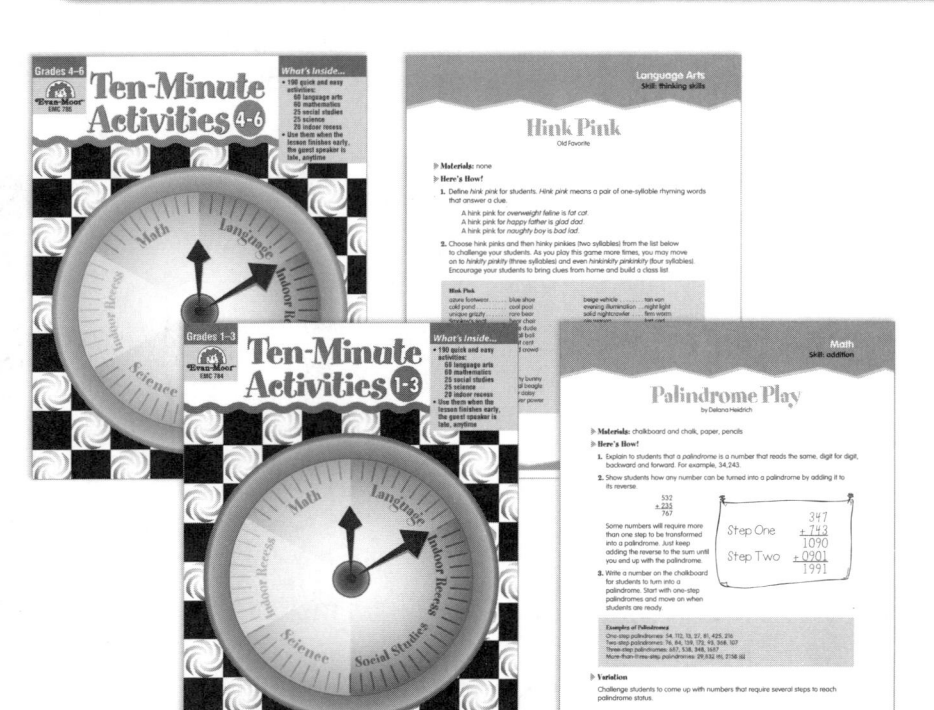

Ten-Minute Activities solves the problem of what to do when you need a quick filler. Here are 190 short activities to use the time productively—60 language arts activities, 60 math activities, 25 social studies activities, 25 science activities, and 20 indoor recess activities. Written by a team of master classroom teachers, this is the book you'll turn to again and again. 192 reproducible pages.

| Grades 1–3 | EMC 784-PRO |
| Grades 4–6 | EMC 785-PRO |

Preview at
www.evan-moor.com